The Life of Karl König

The Life of Karl König

Founder of the Camphill Movement

Regine Bruhn

Floris Books

Publisher's note

This book contains extracts from sources written in the first half of the twentieth century that use outdated language in reference to disabled people. We recommend reading them with an understanding of the era and cultural context in which they were written.

Karl König Archive, Vol 25
Subject: Biography

Series editor: Richard Steel

Karl König's collected works are issued by
The Karl König Institute, Aberdeen
First published in English by Floris Books,
Edinburgh in 2026.

Also available as an eBook

Authorised EU Representative: Easy Access System Europe,
Mustamae tee 50, 10621 Tallinn, Estonia
gpsr.requests@easproject.com
British Library CIP Data available
ISBN 978-183575-013-1

In memory of
Friedwart Bock (1928–2010)

The 'curative-educational attitude' needs to express itself in any social work, in pastoral care, in care for the elderly, in the rehabilitation of mentally ill and physically handicapped people, in the guidance of orphans and refugees, of suicidal and desperate individuals … This is the only answer we have today for a society dancing on the brink of disaster … Only support from person to person – the encounter of a self with another self – the awareness of another individuality without questioning the other's religion, convictions and political background … creates the kind of curative education which can, in a healing way, counteract the threat to the core of humanity. However, this can only work on the strength of profound heart-knowledge.[1]

Karl König
The Child with Special Needs

Contents

Introduction:
The Significance of Vienna for Karl König 9

1. Childhood and Youth (1902–20) 21
2. Higher Education and Training (1920–27) 44
3. The Years in Silesia (1928–35) 62
4. The Viennese Years and Emigration (1936–38) 88
5. Arrival in Scotland (1938–40) 115
6. Camphill: Building a Community (1941–44) 134
7. Developments and Transformations (1945–63) 160
8. The Last Years (1963–66) 189

Acknowledgements 207

Notes 209

Bibliography 227

Index 231

Introduction

The Significance of Vienna for Karl König

Karl König, doctor, curative educator, community builder and founder of the Camphill Movement, was born in Vienna to a Jewish family on September 25, 1902. His birthplace was to have a profound effect on him, shaping his early life and exerting an influence over him long after he left, fleeing persecution from the Nazis.

At the beginning of the twentieth century, Vienna was the capital of the Austro-Hungarian Empire and one of Europe's most important cities. The cosmopolitan city was a microcosm of the multi-ethnic state in which the inhabitants of sixteen nations, each with their own language and culture, lived side by side. Such complex, cultural coexistence held many difficulties and challenges, but for the young König – who experienced more than his fair share of adversity – it offered numerous opportunities and a firm foundation for his life's task. When the first curative educational community was established under his guidance on the Camphill Estate near Aberdeen (later to become the worldwide Camphill Movement) the memory of this formerly diverse and tolerant city influenced his ideal of community building. Indeed, throughout his life, König felt a longing for his original home. As he wrote in his 'Autobiographical Fragment': 'Vienna was so different!'[1]

Life in the city at the turn of the twentieth century had become much safer since the damming of the Danube a few decades earlier. The tram network, the hospitals and the municipal water, gas and electricity supplies were among the most modern in Europe. For König, Vienna was a place where the East and West met.[2]

Vienna was home to a vibrant cultural life: there were museums and galleries for the fine arts, the Burgtheater, the national theatre of Austria, and the State Opera. It was also the city of music: Mozart, Haydn, Beethoven, Schubert, Brahms and Mahler had all worked there. Their melodies resounded in bourgeois as well as aristocratic circles, in concert halls and churches. The dances, especially the Viennese waltzes by Johann Strauss and others, conquered not only the ballrooms but also the dance floors of the common people. Vienna was a city of science with an important university and took a leading position in medicine and physics, but also in philosophy.

Vienna also had a rich bohemian life, and those who were artistically inclined met in salons and coffee houses similar to Paris to exchange their latest compositions and poetry. Fine, elegant living went hand in hand with a mixture of traditional polite manners and informal cordiality. The famous Viennese charm was expressed especially in the dialect that connected the different social classes, but also in an ambience of traditional homeliness with its variety of local pastries, the *heurigen* wine[3] and, finally, the popular atmosphere of the historic public park and entertainment district known as the Prater with its famous amusement park. In the art and architecture of Vienna modernism began to assert itself and take its place alongside the old traditions. A grand boulevard, the Ring, had emerged with many representative buildings, a Greek-style parliament building, and a statue of Pallas Athena, which inspired König to later write: 'Did a Greek spirit not waft through the city…? Had not Athens arisen once more in a Central European guise…?'[4]

In the last third of the nineteenth century, people of the most diverse origins from all over the Habsburg Empire had moved to Vienna, including many Jews who had been persecuted by pogroms in Eastern Europe. They were hoping for better living and working conditions and social advancement in this cosmopolitan and tolerant city. At the beginning of the twentieth century, more Jews lived here than in any other major European city. These were people from very different social backgrounds, ranging from those who were integrated into the middle and upper classes to beggars and pedlars from Eastern Europe. Since being given legal equality in 1868, Jews in Austria had experienced a growing emancipation and participation in social life.[5] Now administrative, intellectual and artistic professions were more open to them. This was the beginning of a golden age whose development was largely of Jewish origin. However, such progress also led to a rise in antisemitism, which came partly from Catholic circles, partly from circles critical of capitalism, and was then intensified by the mass immigration of Russian and Polish Jews after the first Russian revolution in 1905.

Karl König was born in Vienna's 2nd district, known as Leopoldstadt, a Jewish-influenced, petit-bourgeois district with many narrow streets. His grandparents had only recently come to Vienna with their families at the end of the nineteenth century: on his mother's side from Moravia and on his father's side from Burgenland, Austria's easternmost state. König would later write of this generation:

> At this time thousands of Jewish and non-Jewish citizens of the Austro-Hungarian Empire were streaming to the imperial city from many crown lands, from Bohemia and Hungary, Silesia and

The view along Taborstrasse, one of the oldest and most important streets in Vienna's 2nd district, Leopoldstadt, where Karl König was born.

> Galicia, from Carniola and Moravia. They hoped not only to find better earning opportunities in this growing metropolis but also to gain a higher social position; they all wanted to be respected citizens.[6]

König's parents, too, were both working in order to pay off their recently acquired shoe shop as soon as possible.

König was born with a deformity of his feet, and although he received treatment, doctors were only able to alleviate his condition not eliminate it entirely. This led to a lifelong walking impairment. Just like his parents, König was very short of stature: as an adult he never measured more than 4ft 11in (150cm). In his early years he was cared for by a nanny, who often took him to visit Vienna's many Catholic churches during their outings together. In a way, this was the first step on König's journey out of the religious traditions of his father's formerly Orthodox Jewish family. His friendship with the sons of another

Karl König's parents standing in the doorway of their shoe shop with their employees.

Jewish family, who were already more integrated into bourgeois Viennese life, enabled him to transfer, at the age of eleven, to a *Realgymnasium,* a type of secondary school with a focus on modern languages, maths and sciences. Although the school was outside his district, the distance to his new school was not much greater than to his previous one. Nevertheless, when the young Karl König left Leopoldstadt in the mornings and crossed the bridge over the Danube Canal, it was as if he was entering a new world.

This experience provided him with an entry into the arts and culture of Vienna, to education and science, which gave rise in him to many religious, philosophical, social and political questions. He was especially drawn to socialism, Christianity and, eventually, anthroposophy. He was influenced by Vienna's cosmopolitan tolerance, the artistic avant-garde and the charming way of life of the time. This influence remained throughout his life, complementing his seriousness as a natural scientist, anthroposophist, researcher, doctor, curative teacher and social reformer.

König's first experience outside his Austrian homeland was in Switzerland, where he spent a few months in 1927 as an assistant doctor to Ita Wegman in the anthroposophical clinic she had founded in Arlesheim near Basel.[7] The clinic was close to the Goetheanum, the world headquarters of the Anthroposophical Society in Dornach. König gave his first public lectures there, some of which were received positively.[8] Ira Wegman gave the young Viennese doctor a great deal of encouragement and understanding. She was a multilingual Dutch woman who had grown up in Indonesia, had a lot of experience of the world and maintained international contacts in the most diverse circles. With antisemitism on the rise, she became increasingly concerned for the safety of König and other Jewish colleagues; through her diplomatic and political contacts she would eventually help König to flee into exile in Scotland.[9]

König spent his first professional years, from 1928 to 1935, near Breslau, now the Polish city of Wrocław, in Silesia, where he was the medical director of Pilgramshain, a newly founded curative educational home. He was able to make many personal and professional contacts there, especially through his efforts to spread anthroposophical work. Silesia, which is now predominantly Polish, had temporarily been part of the Habsburg Empire, but in the early part of the twentieth century belonged to Germany. In January 1933, the National Socialists took power. In the weeks and months that followed, they began to eliminate the democratic structures of the Weimar Republic, which has been founded in 1919 after the First World War, and to establish their inhuman practices of discrimination, persecution and extermination.

Several characteristics of Karl König had to be a thorn

in the side of the new rulers: his Jewish origin, his short stature and walking disability, his political views, influenced by socialism, and his anthroposophical worldview, whose holistic and individualistic image of the human being fundamentally contradicted Nazi ideology. Added to this was König's medical and curative educational commitment to children 'in need of special care of the soul',[10] who were mostly categorised by the Nazis as 'life unworthy of life'.[11] They were soon to be forcibly sterilised or murdered. Representatives of anthroposophical institutions often tried to negotiate with the Nazi authorities for the continuation and recognition of their work, but König's Jewish origins were not negotiable.[12] This led to increasing discrimination and, eventually, with the introduction of the Nuremberg Race Laws, to disenfranchisement. Nevertheless, despite the possibilities for work becoming more and more restricted, Karl König remained an astonishingly long time in Silesia before returning to Vienna in the spring of 1936. At the time, Austria was still an independent country, although it wouldn't be for much longer.

Vienna had greatly changed in König's absence. After the First World War it had been governed by the Social Democratic Party. Then, in the spring of 1934, representatives of corporative statism and so-called Austrofascism, supported by the Italian dictator Benito Mussolini, came to power. Karl König spent two and a half years in Vienna with his family. During this time, his wife, Tilla, gave birth to their fourth and final child. After some initial difficulties, König succeed not only in establishing a very successful medical practice, but also in attracting a large social circle through his public lecturing activities. Out of this a group of young people emerged who would later form the core of the new Camphill community.

When the Nazis seized power in Vienna on March 11, 1938, it was completely different from their takeover of Berlin in January 1933. In Germany, there had been a gradual process of intimidation and violence. The various measures discriminating against and ousting Jews from public life had proceeded in stages over a long period of time, escalating into disenfranchisement, deprivation, persecution and, ultimately, murder. In Vienna, however, the terror began immediately. The midday train to Prague was the last to leave Austria unchecked, and by that evening masses of people had crowded into Vienna's railway stations attempting to flee. From now on Austria was called Ostmark and was to be transformed into a model state of the SS, the Nazi Party's elite guard. The police and security apparatus were transformed from day one to suit the Nazis. The German Propaganda Ministry distributed millions of leaflets as well as cheap, mass-produced radios, so-called *Volksempfänger.*

Within the first few days, Viennese Jews were forced to clean walls and street pavements, removing political slogans by hand. After two weeks, this 'spontaneous' aggression ended and was replaced by bureaucratically regulated reprisals designed to feign legitimate action. The Nuremberg Race Laws were introduced retroactively to the day of the seizure of power. In the first week of the so-called *Anschluss* of Austria, there were at least 600 suicides; by the end of that month, about 70,000 people had been arrested. The 'Viennese model' of aggressive humiliation of the Jews became the model for Nazi pogroms in all parts of the German Reich during Kristallnacht, the Night of Broken Glass, on November 9–10, 1938.[13]

In 1938, around 170,000 Jews lived in Vienna, of whom about 65,000 would be murdered in the Holocaust.[14] Many, especially younger people, managed to emigrate in time. Karl König's wife had no Jewish background, so she and their four children were not in any immediate danger.

König himself was able to flee Austria with the help of an Italian patient.

In many ways, the expulsion of the Jews made Vienna a city without a soul because the Jewish population had embodied ethnic, religious and cultural diversity. As Manfred Flügge wrote in his book on Vienna of 1938:

> In March 1938, not only the soul of Vienna was lost. The last refuge of German intellectual freedom also fell, a peak of literary criticism, creativity, knowledge, philosophy and daring courage, along with its very own kind of humour. Lost was the glittering constellation of the metropolises of Prague, Berlin, Budapest with their secret centre in Vienna, which gave all writing, activity, poetry, music-making and drama not only a framework but also style and spice. Everything that could be emulated of the lost city, Vienna as a spiritual, sensual, stylish way of life, capable of openness, joining together and understanding ... all this was saved and transplanted into all the world by the exiles and outcasts and preserved for posterity.[15]

For König, Vienna, along with Prague, would always symbolise the heart of Central Europe, which he wished to preserve from the barbarism that had befallen Europe. König carried Vienna in his soul as his inner home in the external homelessness of exile, and the Viennese spirit of diversity and tolerance would have a profound effect on the community he would later found. Many other Viennese emigrants fared no different from him in their own way: like König, they wanted to save the special spirit of Vienna.

Through Ita Wegman's mediation, König was granted an entry permit to Great Britain. After weeks in Italy, Switzerland and France, he finally arrived in London, the first real place of refuge for him in exile. How different it was from Vienna. How different then was Scotland, where first Kirkton House and then the Camphill Estate near Aberdeen offered König, his family and the founding group the opportunity to initiate a curative educational community. Soon the first children in need of special care arrived, initially only from German-speaking emigrant families, then also from Great Britain. At the same time, settling in proved to be a challenge. They all found themselves in the far north, by the sea, in a completely different, cooler and wetter climate. They were surrounded by a culture that was new to them with its own history, and confronted with a foreign language and manners that were unfamiliar.

König described these experiences as follows:

> Whether town or metropolis, village or hamlet, each has its own 'face' and is unlike any other – it has its own individuality. Its unique features are shaped by the memories of all the events and activities that have taken place in its houses and streets, gardens and avenues, at its squares and fountains, gates and towers ... Nevertheless, everyone who has grown up or grown old there carries a part of it within themselves. Such a 'personality of place' expresses itself through the way we speak, the particular melody of our gestures and in the unique colours of our experiences and perceptions. And when arriving in a foreign city to settle and live, it is not easy to harmoniously integrate one's own gestures – already acquired in a previous daily existence – into the new way of life with its quite different rhythms. It was like that for many of us who were taken away from Vienna and Austria to the north of Scotland ... Vienna was so different![16]

When the Second World War broke out, the situation was aggravated by the fact that König and the other founding members of Camphill were initially regarded as 'enemy aliens'.

At end of the war, when it was no longer necessary to remain in exile, König and the members of the community chose to remain in Scotland. From there they carried their Central European impulse to various countries across the world through the founding of new Camphill communities. To König's great joy this also became possible in Central Europe itself, not in Austria at first, but near Lake Constance, which was bordered by Germany, Austria and Switzerland. The region had once been part of the Habsburg Empire, and it was here, in Brachenreuthe near Überlingen, that König would spend the last years of his life.

On the occasion of their twenty-fifth wedding anniversary, in the spring of 1954, König and his wife visited Vienna. It was his first time back since leaving the city in 1938. A few days later König summed up his impressions in a letter to a friend:

> And then there was Vienna; well, it was strange and somehow also beautiful to wander through the places of one's youth and one's spirit awakening. To see again the streets and houses through which one has carried much pain and much joy, and above all to be allowed to experience again the infinite magic of the landscape.[17]

During a stay in October 1963, he felt a stronger relationship and wrote in his diary: 'Now a real connection has been made, and the ground has been laid for further work here.'[18]

Another visit to Vienna, also with courses and lectures,

became possible the following year, as did a trip to Bohemia. But his further hopes and plans for an expansion of his work to other countries in the eastern part of Central Europe did not come about.

Karl König died on March 27, 1966.

1
Childhood and Youth (1902–20)

The boy

Karl König, named after his paternal grandfather, was the only child of Adolf Aron Ber and Bertha König, née Fischer. Their flat in the house at Rotensterngasse 4 was in Leopoldstadt, the 2nd district of Vienna, which was home to many Jews who had moved to the steadily growing capital of the Habsburg Empire at the time of industrialisation.

As an adult, König would write about Leopoldstadt:

> This was no ghetto, but a unique district of lanes and alleyways where Jewish people striving for emancipation had found their place. One family lived there like any other; they were all minor businessmen and tradesmen, employees or civil servants. They shared in common not only their outward life circumstances but also a kind of inner attitude, which gave them all the same inner mood of soul. They felt themselves to be Jews – albeit emancipated; nonetheless still Jews, who belonged to the chosen people and who in every respect felt themselves to be above all other people who were *goyim*, Gentiles. The Jews were distinguished by a quite particular pride.[1]

During the twelve-day postpartum period, König's mother was kept in the dark about the fact that her son had been born with clubfeet: because of insufficiently developed tendons, both feet were twisted inwards. A specialist recommended massages and bandages, which the boy had to wear at night. In her memoirs, Bertha described the child's heartbreaking screams as his tendons were massaged.[2] She attributed this condition to a fall she had suffered from a ladder in her shoe shop during the fifth month of pregnancy.

Karl made steady progress, however. By the age of one, he had learned to stand flat on the soles of his feet with support, and by the time he was fifteen-months old had learned to walk relatively well on his own, helped initially by a three-legged walking frame his parents had bought him. It was agreed that no surgery was needed. Although König's parents ran their own shoe shop with a large selection of models and sizes, their son's shoes had to be custom-made of deerskin with steel splints on the sides. König would wear orthopaedic shoes throughout his life.

Bertha became pregnant again but unfortunately suffered a miscarriage. She would not have another child. From then on, Bertha's attention was very much focused on her only son. He was well-behaved and made very good progress in his development: by the age of two, Karl spoke in complete sentences and was able to engage in polite conversation.

The parental home

König's parents both came from Jewish families. His father had a strict Orthodox upbringing, while his mother's family were less observant and only celebrated special holidays.

König's father, Adolf Aron Ber König, was seven years

Bertha König with her son, Karl.

older than his wife, Bertha, and came from Kobersdorf in Burgenland. The König family belonged to the Jewish tribe of Levi, the hereditary priestly class in ancient Israel who had been responsible for serving in the Temple and implementing the cultic purity commandments. After Adolf's father suffered an accident, the family moved to Vienna in 1878 in search of better medical care. They ran a small general store in Leopoldstadt where Jewish Orthodox life was concentrated. However, because Adolf König did not place himself within the strict Orthodox tradition, his family eventually broke off contact with him. Nevertheless, he continued to be influenced by his Levitical upbringing. He was considered serious, silent, kind and wise, was very well read and owned an extensive library.[3]

Karl's mother, Bertha Fischer, was born in 1880 in Iglau, Moravia, which was then part of the Austro-Hungarian Empire (it is now Jihlava in the Czech Republic). She was the second youngest daughter of nine siblings. Despite her father working as a ladies' tailor, the family had little money, and all the children had to go out to work as soon as possible. They lived in poor conditions in a tenement building: their flat had only one bedroom with a large kitchen. In her memoirs, Bertha described how three children shared one bed, a fact that she took for granted. Life was difficult and not without tragedy. When Bertha was just three-and-a-half years old, her fifteen-year-old sister died suddenly of typhoid. But despite these hardships, Bertha recalled her childhood as a happy one, with moments of contentment and harmony. She did not remember her parents ever quarrelling.[4]

The family moved to Vienna in 1886. When Bertha finished school, she found an apprenticeship as a seamstress before later being offered a job in a local branch of a large shoe shop owned by a cousin. It wasn't long before she held a well-paid, responsible position. It was here that she met her future husband, who worked as a manager in the main shop. Once a week Adolf König came to the branch to do the accounts. It must have been love at first sight, and from then on, the two of them met secretly at lunchtime in a nearby park, ate their sandwiches, and dreamed of their wedding. All this had to be kept secret because, according to the custom of the time, Bertha's older sisters were to be married first. They found a way out, however, through their professional situation: they were offered their own branch of the Bauer shoe company to run in Glockengasse, with the possibility of buying the business after a few years. Under these circumstances, Bertha's father agreed to her marrying Adolf König, and he arranged the wedding in the Jewish religious community for September 24, 1901.

Bertha and Adolf continued working after the birth of their son to pay off the shoe shop as soon as possible, so Karl spent a lot of time with his nanny, known as 'Fräulein'. Although his parents had assimilated into Viennese society, they still observed the high Jewish festivals, and little Karl prayed with them in Hebrew at home and attended synagogue.[5] König's nanny, however, was Catholic and when he was six years old, she took him to church on Easter Sunday. During Holy Week, an Easter mountain with a tomb was set up there. Just as the birth of Jesus was recreated in a nativity scene during Advent and Christmas, the Passion, death and resurrection of Christ were visually reconstructed. Six-year-old Karl looked at everything carefully. He wanted to take a closer look at the empty Easter tomb, but was forbidden from doing so because only the priest was allowed to look inside. When Karl came home, he announced that he wanted to become a priest. When everyone laughed and explained that this was impossible for him as a Jew, he concluded – quite logically in his understanding – that he wanted to become a rabbi. As a teenager, looking back on that moment, he wrote in his diary: 'From now on I lived piously, as befitted a prospective rabbi.'[6]

As soon as Karl was old enough, his father took him to the Prater on Sundays. The boy enjoyed these excursions to the large park nearby, especially to the Wurstelprater, the amusement park, as he otherwise experienced his father as a rather quiet and reserved man.[7]

School days

In 1908, Karl started school nearby in Obere Augartenstrasse. His nanny accompanied him on the way there and back. On his first day, his teacher greeted him with the words: 'What have we here, what kind of little squirt is this?'[8]

During this period, König's mother described him as a quiet child who liked to leaf through his books and was soon able to read. An early favourite of König's was the book *Robinson Crusoe* by Daniel Defoe. He also learned to read and write Hebrew in preparation for his Bar Mitzvah, the festival that takes place on the first Sabbath after a Jewish boy's thirteenth birthday, and that marks him becoming a full member of his community. When he wasn't studying and being a model pupil, König was very helpful in the shoe shop: 'He was happy when he could be with us in the shop,' his mother later wrote. 'He would climb the ladder and always bring me the right shoe if I needed to serve a customer.'[9]

On his way to school, the young König passed a care home run by the city of Vienna for the poor, the sick and the old. Above the entrance it read: 'Whatever you did for one of the least of these brothers and sisters of mine, you did for me.'[10]

Karl König later discovered this saying was from the Gospel of Matthew in the Christian New Testament (Matt.

The care home in Vienna which the young Karl König passed on his way to school.

25:40). The verse made a deep impression on him, as it seemed different from the laws he had learned in his Jewish religious education. When he was eleven years old, König's mother found a picture of Christ on the inside of his wardrobe door. She later wrote:

> And so he grew up. We knew that he was regularly going to church, but we did not talk to him about it, we thought that this was just a phase he was going through at this stage of his life.[11]

Reflections on this inscription and other religious questions accompanied König during his school years. His original understanding of God as an old man with a white beard changed. A few years later, he described his religious experiences from that time:

> God … became blurred, he became big, a man; whom you can't see because of his size. Then I

> began to see and to feel. I saw nature in all its beauty and glory. And then it became apparent to me: this is God. Nature is God. I had formed my own religion. A religion of nature that I now live by. I pray when I see. I see God in everything.[12]

After his first four years at primary school, Karl went to a nearby secondary school, which focused more on a mathematical and scientific education. His mother remembered:

> He was now 11 years old. He had his own study for we now had moved into a larger apartment in the same building in which the business was located. We bought new furniture, genuine carpets, beautiful pictures and an Ehrbach grand piano because he could already play quite beautifully. He had an extensive library, Schiller, Goethe, also Schopenhauer and Kant and various other masters. When he started secondary school, we had to dismiss the nanny; however, we kept our dear and beloved cook who had been with us for the last 20 years. We took a tutor for him in the afternoons. On one occasion my son said to me: 'Mother you should pay me the salary you give to my tutor as he's not teaching me, I'm teaching him.'[13]

König did not feel comfortable at the secondary school. About his school years he later wrote: 'In some things I was rather headstrong and so my attendance of primary and secondary school was not without problems.'[14]

As a child, he often felt lonely. Apart from the children in the wider family, he had no friends the same age. He felt like an outsider because of the problem with his feet:

A silhouette of Karl König from the Adria Exhibition in Vienna, 1913.

> From birth I was afflicted with a foot condition, I was clumsy in games, could not walk far and hardly run at all! I was laughed at and was therefore withdrawn and did not take part in other children's games. And since mostly children become friends at play, I remained alone.[15]

He eventually made friends with Alfred and Arthur Bergel, whose family were part of his parents' circle of acquaintances. After an argument with a teacher, König asked his mother to let him transfer to the secondary school in Glasergasse in the 9th district of Alsergrund, which Alfred and Arthur both attended.

His mother wrote:

> One day he came to me and said: 'Mother, I am not going back to this school, I had an argument with my professor and I will ... have to be moved to school district 9. My two good friends, the Bergels, are there and we shall be together.' Well, the school change was not quite so simple ... This might appear easier than it actually was for he was faced with a strange school and new professors. At first he was not happy as he had only his two friends, the Bergels, to help him. We became very friendly with the Bergel family.[16]

Karl König was barely twelve years old when the First World War broke out. His mother later wrote in her memoir:

> Now the First World War broke out. We were staying for the summer in Kierling – on this occasion ... the Bergels were staying in our apartment. We returned immediately to Vienna and

At the Bergels. Front row from left: Marianne and Alfred Bergel, and Stephanie Korolanyi (the name of the young boy at the end of the front row is unknown). Back row from left: Ludwig Korolanyi and Karl König. Stephanie and Ludwig were König's cousins.

> from that point a change came about in our young one. He wanted no new clothes and was always looking for washed out clothes indicating that he was ashamed to go out on the street well-dressed when people were experiencing such a misery. It was a difficult task for us knowing how to act in such circumstances. People who we knew came to the shop and asked why we let our young one go about so shabbily dressed, observing: 'You are well off and can afford such clothes.' We said that it was his wish and there was nothing we could do about it. Often, he came home in winter without his overcoat. When we asked where he had left it, he would reply: 'I saw a poor young person freezing without a coat, so I gave him mine.'[17]

At the age of thirteen, Karl König celebrated his Bar Mitzvah, which allowed him to fulfil the religious duties of a Jew from that day on. These included reading from the Torah, the Jewish book of teachings, and also putting on the so-called tefillin, the leather capsules that contain passages from the Torah on parchment and which are fastened to the hand and head with leather straps. Later, his mother recalled the Haftara, his first public reading in the synagogue, but also his own speech, which already pointed to his independent path in religious matters:

> We ... remembered ... how at 13 he had been confirmed, how wonderfully he spoke from the Haftara, how small he was at 13 and how beautiful the ceremony in the house had been. All our relations and many good friends had come, he had given a wonderful speech that he had put together himself and in which he highly praised his parents. He gave thanks to us that he had been allowed to go his own way.[18]

The König family did not have to suffer hardship during the first years of the First World War as shoes could be exchanged for food. The young König could hardly bear this in view of the general misery: 'Again and again our son would ask: "Why do we eat so well, when other people go hungry?"'[19] He gave away his pocket money.

Youth and friendships

The war shaped Karl König's youth from 1914 to 1918. He later described this time:

> Then the First World War arrived and brought along with it the fall of the Austro-Hungarian monarchy. I clearly remember the day when King Franz Joseph was entombed in the Capuchin crypt and then two years later – I was just sixteen years old – the collapse of the front and the November Revolution of 1918. At that time, I became intensely occupied with philosophical, scientific and social questions: the loss of all previously existing values called for new norms and attitudes. In this striving, however, I had no support or guidance from my parents.[20]

This must have been a difficult time for his parents, too. It was not easy accompanying their son during this phase, especially as he probably also suffered from serious depressive moods. As his mother wrote:

> I must return to the progress of my son who was causing us such worry. It was still wartime and he was in his seventeenth year, the change in his life was truly remarkable. He very much drew into himself; he suffered from migraines which often meant spending several days in bed. He spent most of his evenings with the Bergels. We often went to the theatre or the coffee house, but he never wanted to go with us. We used to return anxious and with a heavy heart. It was a sad time for him for he seemed to be bearing all the troubles of the world. We were afraid to open the door not knowing what state he would be in. Perhaps he was alone too much; we just did not know how to act. We knew that he went regularly to church, but we left him to his own desires, for I believed that was for him the best way.[21]

König enjoyed the atmosphere in the art-loving Bergel family, with whom he spent a lot of time playing music. He developed a deep friendship with Alfred who was the same age. Alfred, or Fredi as he was known, had a talent for painting and could be found drawing in any kind of situation.[22] The two attended the same class, had mutual acquaintances and friends and were able to exchange ideas about art, friendship and love, but also about religion. In a diary entry for July 6, 1918, Karl König recalled their first in-depth conversation:

> It was on 15 March of that year. We had just finished school at 4 o'clock and I asked Fredi (a colleague) to go for a walk with me ... And there we started talking about Schopenhauer: in relation to women. But we knew little about each other and didn't quite dare to make our views known. Then I took heart and told him about my religious doubts. At that time, I had to put on tefillin (prayer straps). I did not know why I should do this; I only did it out of reverence for my parents. I told him that. Then he became more trusting. He told me about his love for my cousin ... I told him about myself and we talked for three hours. By then we got to know each other inside and out. We understood each other and one felt for the other. And so we became friends.[23]

Together they attended theatre performances, concerts and operas. König still went to the Prater frequently as a youth, especially with Alfred and Alfred's father, Arnold, who had a great interest in all aspects of culture in addition to being a merchant.

Arnold Bergel knew many of the showmen and artists who worked in the Wurstelprater. He had especially good contacts with the actors of the show booths and theatres, even writing short plays or jokes for them. The Bergel sons and Karl König were sometimes allowed to take on roles. The sixteen-year-old König was so inspired by this that he began to write his own short plays. He submitted these to Arnold Bergel, who gave him advice on how to develop his own style.[24]

This interest stayed with König throughout his life. As an adult he wrote a number of plays for the annual festivals celebrated by the members of Camphill communities, and wrote poetry to express his feelings.[25]

The sixteen-year-old König described his relationship with art:

> Art is a big, big garden … I started learning to play the piano in class four. I disliked music very much at that time … Time passed, I went to secondary school. But now I started going to the theatre … I went to almost every classical performance and was thus introduced to literature.[26]

The adolescent was impressed by the writings of Shakespeare, Schiller, Goethe, Ibsen, Hauptmann, Wedekind and Hebbel. In language he experienced an expression of the mind, and with the onset of puberty he found access to music as an expression of feeling. He wrote about a performance he went to see of Wagner's *Meistersinger* and the profound effect it had on him:

> What I felt I cannot describe. It was the first great piece of music I heard. I went for a walk for a full hour after the end to calm myself down, because I was boiling inside so strongly, I would like to say, close to overflowing. And from then on, music was the most important thing to me … Now playing

> the piano was no longer a nuisance, now it was a pleasure ... I went to the opera every week.[27]

In 1918, during the last summer of the war, the König and Bergel families spent their summer holidays in Kierling near Klosterneudorf, a popular resort about 7½ miles (12 kilometres) from Vienna, between the Danube and the Vienna Woods. Such 'summer retreats' were customary in Vienna at the time. As a young boy, before the war, König had travelled to the countryside in the summer with his parents and the family of his father's older sister. They would rent a holiday flat together and live harmoniously like one big family. Adolf König would work at the shoe shop during the week and join his family at the weekend, as was traditional, but Bertha König also went to the shop every day, leaving Karl with his aunt. Karl had felt at home with his aunt's family and was very attached to his two slightly older cousins, Hans and Karl.

During that last summer of the war, Karl stayed with relatives or with the Bergel family the whole time. There were garden parties, hikes and walks at night, and with his friend Alfred he had lively exchanges about serious matters, including their first experiences of falling in love. They played music and sang together. The war seemed far away. Back in Vienna, the young man did not find it easy to be alone again, especially in the face of the horror and hardship of the war. On the following weekends, Karl and the Bergel brothers Alfred and Arthur, known as Fredi and Lolo, visited their carefree holiday resort in Kierling to get food that was no longer available in the city:

> Just yesterday I went to the Bergels'. I couldn't stand it any longer. I had become so used to the family in the summer. I missed Fredi a lot the last few days. Well, I was there and when leaving I felt more light-

> hearted than when I had arrived. We sang again and remembered Kierling. Again, I noticed: he is my best friend. Today, just today, I love him so much. Tomorrow we will go to Kierling together.[28]

Religious and social questions

König's memoirs and diary entries from this time also bear witness to his grappling with religious questions: from his Jewish heritage and his growing interest in Christianity, to his fascination with Far Eastern religions and his search for the spiritual in nature:

> Therefore I was dependent upon books and without anyone to supervise me I studied the most colourful variety: Haeckel and Freud were read with the same devotion as Stefan George and Hugo von Hofmannsthal, Buddha and Lao-tzu, Dumas and Balzac. Around this time, I also discovered the New Testament and in this moment … I felt I had met something that I had long been searching for and that my life would be deeply influenced by it from that point onwards.[29]

König often had religious experiences in nature, as he records in this diary entry from July 1918:

> And again, I was in the mood to pray as a Jew and to fight and suffer for my Jewish religion. And I wanted to be alone. I went to a large meadow and there I saw again the beauty and splendour of nature and saw God as nature. I was strengthened again in my faith in nature.[30]

In his diaries, König commented several times on his struggle with the strict rules of Judaism. On the occasion of the Jewish New Year in September 1918, he wrote:

> It's dreadful. The holidays are in three days. I'll have to go to the temple, spend almost the whole day there, act against my innermost feelings. It will be terrible. But I have to do it, out of reverence for my parents.[31]

He dared to write on the actual holiday, against the strict commandments that governed festivals and the Sabbath:

> Today is Rosh Hashanah and I am writing, this is a dare, I have never written on this high holiday. I must free myself from all these old things of religion. I suffered terribly in the temple when I was still a child and pious. I piously went to the house of God by the hand of my father, father noticed it, I could not pray, I felt terribly sorry for my father, he brought me up in his religion, and now his son had become a heretic. Nature is God, nature gave this to me and will help defend it, I am firm in my faith, what is all this praying for, this bending and kissing, all this foolishness. I asked my father to release me from my temple attendance, [he] refused.[32]

At the end of the ten-day festivities, on the Feast of Atonement, he lamented further:

> And soon [the] Yom Kippur Feast will begin … Two shudderingly bitter days lie ahead. Tomorrow is Fasting Day and Temple Day … I gradually came to talk about religion with my parents. And I only blurted out my views. Of course, my mother told

> me again that anyone who didn't believe in God couldn't be a good person, that the greatest scholars were only Jews, etc. I weakly replied that I didn't believe in God. I only replied weakly, not because I was not sure of myself, but because of my parents. My father regretted that my grandfather/his father was no longer alive, he would surely have converted me again. … I fasted the whole day, not for the sake of religion, but only to test my willpower. I could have eaten, but I did not. I managed to reach my goal in spite of faintness, headache, hunger. I had already been in the temple all day. That was also an achievement.[33]

König was moved by fundamental questions surrounding Jewish identity and the way the Jewish people saw themselves:

> I had some disputes with my cousin, a die-hard Zionist, about Judaism. We have completely opposite views. He says we are a people, I say we are only a religious community. The reasoning is too long for me to give here. I am not a Jew, I am a human being, and I profess to be of the race that strives from darkness into light.[34]

His inward approach towards Christianity at this time was a constant, intensifying process. While König had noted in his diary for Epiphany, 1919, 'Christmas passed without influence',[35] he celebrated the following Christmas in his own solemn way:

> Christmas I spent alone, Christmas Eve, rejoicing in the birth of the greatest man, reading a few chapters from the Bible, Christmas poems by Gerhart,

> Storm, Eichendorff, while a small candle burned in my cupboard, decorated with greenery.[36]

During Holy Week, 1919, he attended the opera: 'Yesterday I went to see *Parzival* … Shall I say it was marvellous? It is, after all, my soul and my spirit … Good Friday magic, the revelation of the Grail.'[37] The following year he wrote:

> The Old Testament preaches 'an eye for an eye, a tooth for a tooth' … It was Christ, the greatest man, who brought ethics into the world. He was the one who made us human … Christ, he was the greatest poet, my future?[38]

At the same time, König's social conscience led to his first political commitment when, in February 1919, he joined the Socialist Middle School Students' Association:

> I am a social democrat altogether. It is precisely because I feel so sorry for people that I became one. Inside, I always have been one … everyone is fighting … for equality, everyone is fighting for the highest. For goodness and humanity. I always fight for it and will probably fight for it until death and maybe beyond.[39]

During this time, König not only cultivated a love of music, especially the operas of Wagner and Mozart, he also read widely, enjoying classical literature as well as more modern, socially critical works. He frequently attended the theatre and was enthusiastic about the plays of Ibsen, Hauptmann and Wedekind.[40] He wrote poetry in these youthful years, too, that gave expression to the hardships he witnessed in his immediate neighbourhood, such as this one:

At noon at the twelfth hour,
When I leave school,
Sitting on a street corner,
A poor blind little Jew.
His violin in his hand,
A fiddle bow plays,
And when I lean towards him,
The little song sounds like a faint breath.[41]

In the summer of 1919, König went on a two-week holiday with his father to Gleichenberg, where they spoke about Judaism and the faith of their forefathers:

> We often go for walks … We understand each other better in silence than in talking. Only sometimes does he tell me about the past. About his past and that of his ancestors … My father tells me about the miraculous work of the Kabbalists, his own experiences or those of his father. I … know nothing. There are so many ambiguities in me. Now I'm looking for … God again.[42]

In October 1919, he noted: 'I have now fully recognised Christ.'[43] König's parents suspected that he had turned away from Judaism. Then, at the beginning of 1920, König wrote about himself in the third person:

> Then he met his father. They walked side by side for a long time and found nothing to talk about. They knew something stood between them … He was alone with his parents. They reproached him for everything … that he was no longer a Jew … And they complained … [how] they suffered greatly because of him … but that his parents could be no friends to him because he was not a good son. He

Karl König (third from left) with the rest of his classmates celebrating the end of school. König's close friend, Alfred Bergel, sits at the other end of the bench.

> saw his father weeping with sorrow at having such a closed-off child, with sorrow at not being able to be a father and a comforter ... And he felt his mother's pain.[44]

During the last two years of school, König studied the writings of Adolf Stöhr, who held a professorship in philosophy and psychology at the University of Vienna. His work centred on questions of cognition and sensual perception. 'For many days and nights,' König wrote, 'I attempted to observe my thinking in order to find a clue to the process of acquiring knowledge.'[45]

Karl König completed his schooling by taking the Matura, the standardised matriculation examination taken by pupils at the end of secondary school in many Central and Eastern European countries. After weighing up his diverse philosophical, artistic and scientific interests, König decided to study medicine. Since he had attended a scientific secondary school, a preparatory year at the University of Vienna was necessary in order to study Latin. While still at school he noted:

> I have now decided to become a medical doctor. I want to help. My life is for humanity, for the great, good humanity that strives for brightness. I am already learning Latin. It gives me great pleasure.[46]

2
Higher Education and Training (1920–27)

At the University of Vienna

In 1920 Karl König began his preparatory year for studying medicine at the University of Vienna. During this time, he continued to live at home. In addition to preparing for his Latin exam, he was already attending lectures on botany, zoology and biology. On the day before his matriculation, he noted his inner attitude and future goals in his diary:

> The sea of materialism will rush in upon me, but I shall stand fast. The world and the universe are full of God and full of angels and wonders, full of goodness and anger and full of will ... My aim will be to go as a doctor from village to village ... to work for what is good and true.[1]

König's scientific studies fascinated him. They raised all manner of questions for which he found answers and inspiration in the writings of the German poet and scientist Johann Wolfgang von Goethe, especially in his ideas on the metamorphosis of plants. König later wrote about this period:

> Now, for the first time, the study of anatomy, embryology and histology could become a daily source of the most profound and heartfelt joy. Bones and muscles revealed new worlds to me. The idea of metamorphosis gripped my attention deeply, and through this I came to know the working of creative formative forces in nature.[2]

As a student König continued to be interested in the great religious and ethical questions of life, questions concerning his relationship to his fellow human beings, his environment and above all to animals. His mother described an incident that probably occurred during his early student days:

> There was one occasion when my son did not come home for the whole night. We thought he might have spent the night with the Bergels. In the morning, he returned dishevelled and dirty. We asked him where he had been. He replied that he had been with the police. Apparently, he had given a speech in the city park saying how badly animals were treated there. The knacker had come to the park in a small cart and in a cruel manner had caught the stray dogs. He had a long thin rope on the end of which was an iron hook, and it was with this that he caught the dogs. He threw the rope so skilfully that he caught the tail of the dog; once caught the poor animal was thrown into the cart and then later destroyed. And there came from the cart a pitiful wailing. So my son gave a speech to a large crowd in the park, something that was strictly forbidden in Vienna. The police came and arrested him and took him away. He was not allowed to call us.[3]

The medical faculty of the University of Vienna was one of the most important in Europe and the first to have its own curative education department. This was a pioneering achievement in which psychiatry, paediatrics, psychology, social science and education worked together. It can be assumed that König encountered this department in the context of paediatrics, as he mentioned attending lectures by Emil Fröschels, the speech scientist and speech therapist who worked there.[4]

Karl König's socialist interests

König's friendship with Alfred Bergel and his circle of friends continued into the first years of his studies. There were many social gatherings in Vienna, and during the summer months of 1921 to 1924 König went on trips with the Bergel family to Kierling, a renowned resort in the Vienna Woods in Lower Austria. Although he took part in many of the hikes organised by his friends, König repeatedly reached the limits of his physical mobility due to his congenital foot condition. When he needed to rest he used the time to read and write, practising an inward mobility of mind rather than an outward one.[5]

In addition, he had joined a kind of *Wandervogel* group within the Austrian Young Socialists.[6] In his diary he noted:

> At that time I was always with the new friends … I only did my work mechanically … My thoughts were always with my friends. We were together evening after evening. We sang, we laughed … at a party in my flat, where we were all masked up, singing, dancing, playing, kissing, until the morning.[7]

Karl König (third from left) on a hiking trip with friends in the mountains, 1927.

König's interests were wide-ranging, and time and again he found other subjects more appealing to him than studying medicine. After his first difficult medical exams, he considered studying agriculture instead:

> I wanted to leave then. I wrote to Norway and applied for a job as a farm labourer. I got it, only I was refused permission to leave the country. Then I was supposed to go down to Italy, but that also failed because of various things. I had to stay in Vienna again. I was without a foothold and didn't know which way to turn. Surrounded by much love and friendship, but weak at heart.[8]

During this period, König kept up a lively correspondence with friends and was occasionally in love, sometimes unhappily, which at times led to depressive moods. Life in the Austrian capital was marked by great social and political upheaval. The end of the Empire had not, by any means, led to a stable democratic republic, but to competing ideological factions of various kinds. König studied Marxist literature and wrote an essay called 'Biology of Socialism', in which he expressed the goal of making people economically free and leading them to knowledge. His diary entries from this period were sporadic and summarised longer periods of time. In the summer of 1924, König travelled with one of his socialist friends through Italy to Sicily, which particularly impressed him:

> The whole landscape gripped me in such a way that after a two-hour journey from Palermo to Messina I could no longer look, but crushed by this beauty and splendour, I had to lie down on the bench in the carriage and could only sleep … What was still important for me was the constant mental exchange with my travelling companion, Nuki. He showed me many things that I had overlooked so far and in a different perspective to how I had seen them until now … Essentially, he showed me many manifestations of capitalism, both in outward cultural existence and in our inner conventionality … I learned to move more freely. I cannot mention everything that was beautiful in Italy. The last farewell from Venice, the wonderful excellent wine and the women in Sicily with their steel-grey eyes, all these are but resting places and not the path, which will be the essential thing.[9]

König also joined a small group of socialist doctors – who were separate from the social democratic student movement – and again considered dropping out of medical school and changing his subjects:

> I ... studied a lot of socialist literature, *Das Kapital,* and was well on the way to switching completely to social sciences. I myself presided over the socialist doctors. It was always a task before my eyes to somehow alleviate the great misery, political and economical, which was taking on exorbitant forms at that time, and to help build the new cultural edifice of socialism.[10]

Karl König's encounter with anthroposophy

König's encounter with anthroposophy was to have a profound and decisive impact on the direction his life would take. Anthroposophy, a spiritual science for the understanding of the human being, had been founded by the Austrian philosopher Rudolf Steiner, and had already provided inspiration in various fields of work. The first Waldorf school had opened in Stuttgart in 1919, anthroposophical medicine was being developed, as were initiatives relating to curative education and biodynamic agriculture. Anthroposophy had also inspired developments in speech, drama, art, music and architecture, and had given rise to a new art of movement called eurythmy. In 1922, The Christian Community was founded as a movement for religious renewal.

König's first experience of anthroposophy may have taken place at the Swedish Israel Mission, an institution that wanted to bring Christianity closer to Jewish people in particular. Lectures and discussion groups were held there dealing with many different topics. In one of the groups, König met the couple Maria and Norbert Glas, both medical doctors. Through them he gained deeper access to anthroposophy. König later wrote in his diary about this moment:

> The first time I was there ... it was nothing new to me. I felt that there was a direction of thought that essentially fitted into mine, which is based on Goethe. If I remember correctly, I actually arrived with great suspicion. I was armed with my whole armoury of exact psychology, natural science and, above all, my social awareness and [my interest in] socialism ... But I felt fired up by this whole environment, my thoughts took on new directions again and I felt that something was speaking to me ... something spiritual, which could perhaps bring the solution to many things ... what these people told me seemed to me to be much more correct than my thoughts and I thought many things in exactly the same way as they did.[11]

Karl König soon felt himself to be both a socialist and an anthroposophist. He saw both views as offering a way out of the chaos of the contemporary situation and yet he felt a conflict between them, like a spiritual struggle within himself. One offered a spiritual view of the world, whereas the other based itself on material determinism:

> I can speak little about these things, I only spoke to two people who had become my guides in anthroposophy, the two Drs Glas, hinting at individual topics. It was [Maria] in particular who showed and helped me most in the early days. I remember the hours when I sat with her in the hospital and presented all my spiritual conflicts in order to get clarification.[12]

In spring 1925 König became a member of the Anthroposophical Society. Unfortunately, his increasingly intense involvement with anthroposophy led to the end of his friendship with Alfred Bergel and the other companions from his youth.

Shortly after that, König visited the Goetheanum, the headquarters of the Anthroposophical Society in Dornach, Switzerland, and spent time there in the Rudolf Steiner Archive. In a letter he wrote to Maria Röschl, the leader of the Youth Section, in September 1925 he said:

> When I first arrived at the hill in Dornach … I became aware that everything is alive here, standing very firmly in the midst of our time, and that I myself may participate in all the truth, beauty and revelation that emanated here. And with that a certain feeling of security came into me and I became aware that for the first time in my life, being a city dweller and moreover a Jew, I had found my home … The most wonderful hours for me were when I could sit in the archives and study, among so many friends dedicated to the same task. From the outside the hammering of the construction work entered; everywhere the activity was the most intense I had ever experienced.[13]

The Vienna Institute of Embryology

During the clinical semesters of his studies, König earned a small additional income by working as a scientific assistant at the Vienna Institute of Embryology, teaching hundreds of students the art of microscopy. He also had the opportunity to examine human embryos in their first weeks of development, which was a completely new field of research at the time and one that König pursued throughout his life. He spent a lot of time in the library and later wrote about his findings and the correspondence he saw between the development of the embryo and the images in the biblical story of creation:

> Then I made a significant discovery: the embryo's sheath organs form first of all; the embryo as such only begins to develop and build itself up later on ... I was able to show that the immense pictures presented in Genesis are mirrored and recapitulated in the phases of human embryonic sheath formation ... For the first time the harmonious synthesis between science and anthroposophical spiritual science had revealed itself to me. This consideration of the 'whole' – the sum of the parts – became fundamental to my principles of work later on.[14]

At the Institute of Embryology, König published the results of a study he had conducted on the effectiveness of homeopathically diluted substances. He was able to prove that frog larvae in increasingly diluted solutions of silver and lead (D1 to D30)[15] underwent different developments. The results of König's investigations were published in the *Archiv für Experimentelle Medizin* and attracted some attention as they were proof of the effectiveness of diluted solutions according to the principle of homeopathy. König was invited to give a lecture at the Vienna Biological Society, which triggered lively discussions due to the effectiveness of homeopathic methods being repeatedly questioned by medical science.

In the spring of 1927, König completed his studies with a doctorate in medicine. He then began his time as an assistant physician at the university's teaching hospital in Klosterneuburg near Vienna. During his breaks, he liked to sit on the terrace of the library of the nearby Cistercian monastery. There, in the shade of the large chestnut trees, he would look out across the flood plains of the river

Danube and the wide plain of the Marchfeld, which bordered Slovakia to the east and Moravia and Bohemia towards the north. This area had been the granary of Austria for centuries. You could see the towers of baroque churches and the Marchfeld castles. Not only had this been the site of important battles – most recently against Napoleon – but Austria's first steam railway had run here. This environment made a definite impression on König, as he later wrote: 'At that time I became clearly conscious – as never before – of my Central European, Austrian identity.'[16]

Around this time, he received an offer from Professor Fischel to habilitate in the field of embryology. Habilitation is the highest academic qualification in many European countries and often serves as a prerequisite for achieving a professorship. Fischel was dean of the medical faculty and assured König of his full support if he would only keep his anthroposophical views to himself. This was out of the question for Karl König.

Ita Wegman

In October 1927, full of self-doubt, König wrote in his diary:

> In such a bad way I lack humility and overview … I always feel a terrible pain [that] I have never had a personal teacher, a person who can guide me and [for] whom I feel reverence. When I wanted to go to Adolf Stöhr's lecture, he had just died. And Rudolf Steiner I never saw in my life, through my own fault.[17]

König always regretted never having taken the opportunity to meet Rudolf Steiner in person.[18] However, his wish for a personal mentor was soon fulfilled. Only a few days after writing that diary entry, König met the physician Ita Wegman for the first time. Along with Rudolf Steiner, Ita Wegman had developed anthroposophical medicine, a new holistic approach to healing, and she was now the director of the clinical therapeutic institute in Arlesheim near the Goetheanum in Dornach.

König's meeting with Ita Wegman occurred when the latter travelled to Vienna for the funeral of Rudolf Steiner's sister, Leopoldine, which took place on 3 November, 1927. König was part of a small delegation of young doctors who met her at the railway station. Later he wrote:

> When I ask myself where to look for the first dim beginnings of the story of Camphill, I see myself standing on the platform of one of the railway stations in Vienna, waiting for a train … I stood there on the platform, reserved and uncomfortable, because with a few friends, I had been invited to welcome Dr Ita Wegman who was coming to Vienna. I had never met her before and constantly asked myself why it was necessary for me to wait for somebody I did not know … She greeted the welcoming party. I was introduced to her, we shook hands and all was over. I left the station very quickly and went home, not knowing what it was all about.[19]

A few days later, at a social event, König had the opportunity to speak with Ita Wegman in private. She asked him some personal questions and invited him to assist her with her work in Arlesheim. Thus, as early as mid-November 1927, König left Vienna and travelled to Arlesheim.

It was around this time that König's parents learned of his conversion to Christianity. His mother described how she and her husband found out:

> Before my son had gone to Switzerland he had asked me to go to the [Jewish congregation] as he urgently needed a document. So I went and asked to obtain the document. The official looked at me very surprised and said: 'Your son no longer belongs to us; he left Judaism four years ago.' I stood very horrified. The official saw my dismay and asked if I felt all right. I told him that there was nothing wrong, but I was wondering how I was going to break the news to my husband. I went home with very mixed feelings; indeed, wondering if I should tell my husband about it at all. However, I decided he had to be told. He took it a lot better than I had and told me that he had known for some time after having found books by Rudolf Steiner in his library.[20]

Mathilde Maasberg

Karl König's move to Arlesheim, a suburb of Basel in Switzerland, led to his first encounter with his future wife:

> On November 7, 1927 – the day of my arrival in Arlesheim[21] – I met the person who was living in an attic room of the same house I had just moved into. This was Miss Tilla Maasberg, who together with her sister, Maria, had recently established a small curative educational institute in the Silesian Eulengebirge.[22]

Mathilde Maasberg – Tilla – was the middle child of seven siblings and was a rather melancholic and shy individual. Her family lived in Gnadenfrei,[23] a settlement of the Herrnhut Brethren (also known as the Moravian Brotherhood), a Christian community that had emerged from the Bohemian-Moravian Brethren's Union.[24] Tilla's father owned a textiles factory that wove material for curtains, bed linen and towels. The family liked to spend much of their free time in their holiday home, known as the *Waldhaus*, the 'forest-house', in nearby Eulengebirge. Towards the end of her schooling, Tilla went to a kind of finishing school where young girls learned how to run a household. But she was unhappy there and left to train as a children's nurse in Berlin, where she particularly enjoyed caring for premature babies. She returned home, at her family's request, to assist her second-eldest sister, Lene, with the birth of her twins. Lene was suffering from tuberculosis and needed help caring for her two older children.

Tilla's eldest sister, Maria, who was a trained social worker, later asked her to start a children's home with her in the *Waldhaus*. The two sisters had recently become members of the newly founded Christian Community in Breslau; they were also interested in anthroposophy and wanted to make it the basis of their educational work. With this mind, Tilla Maasberg went to Arlesheim in November 1927 to attend the training course in curative education, where she met Karl König. As he initially seemed much older than her (in fact, he was six months younger than she was), it took some time for them to get to know each other and become friends.[25]

The Advent Garden

The Sonnenhof, a care home for children at the Arlesheim clinic, also came under the medical direction of Ita Wegman, and soon after König's arrival, she asked him if he would be willing to work there. König agreed, but first found it necessary to familiarise himself with the daily routine of the children and their special needs:

> But here at the Sonnenhof, there were about thirty smaller and bigger children with enormous or tiny heads, with paralysed limbs; some with an empty gaze; others traumatised by fits. But all of them were children! They laughed and cried; they were joyful and suffered pain like all other children … Consequently, when Dr Wegman asked if I would be prepared to spend a part of my day working at the Sonnenhof as a doctor, I willingly agreed. I was instantly drawn to these children and they quickly became very dear to me. And so I spent many hours with them, learning to dress and undress them, to clean them, to play with them, to calm or encourage them and to be their friend.[26]

It was here, on the first Advent Sunday, that Karl König had an experience which he repeatedly described as the moment in which he recognised his life's task. It happened in what was called the Advent Garden, and was an event that had originated in the Lauenstein care home in Jena, Germany, the first anthroposophical curative education establishment. Some of the curative teachers there had set up a moss garden in the form of a spiral, with candles set into apples on a table. At the Christmas meeting of the Anthroposophical Society in Dornach in 1923, Rudolf Steiner was asked during a break about this practice. He advised them to make the spiral larger and more accessible on the floor so the children could walk around it and experience it with their whole body.[27]

In the very first weeks of his work in Arlesheim, Karl König was able to experience one of the first Advent gardens. There are two impressive descriptions of this decisive event in his life. The first is an essay König wrote in English in 1961 called 'Candle on the Hill'.[28] The second is an account he gave originally in German a few months before his death in 1965:

> The first Advent Sunday soon arrived, a festival that had been completely unknown to me in Catholic Vienna, and one I had never before celebrated. In the afternoon I went to the Sonnenhof to be with the children and there I found a group of co-workers and children gathered together. They sat along the walls in the biggest room in the house. In the middle of the space there was a small mound made out of green moss and earth and a candle was burning on top of it. A spiral marked out with moss lead to the small mound. Every child was given an apple upon which a small candle was fixed. Advent and Christmas songs were sung and one child after another attempted – alone or with help – to walk through the moss spiral to reach the central mound so that they could light their own candle from the main candle. I was profoundly surprised to behold the earnestness and joy with which each child approached the task. There was the great candle! Each small candle attached to an 'apple of sin' had to be lit from this 'proclaiming' Christmas light! And suddenly I knew: 'Yes, this is my future task!' To awaken in each one of these children their own spirit light which would lead

The Advent Garden in Camphill Hall.

> them to their humanity: 'Yes, that is what I want to do!' I am no longer able to say whether my decision was particularly conscious that Advent Sunday, but my heart felt so fulfilled that tears just poured from my eyes and I had to leave the hall. Since then these people have been my *raison d'être*.[29]

Karl König's lecturing activities

Ita Wegman soon recognised König's many talents. At the Christmas Conference in Dornach in 1927 she asked him to give a talk on his special research topic: the origin and development of the human embryo and its connection to the six days of creation in Genesis. The young doctor had to stand on a box to be able to look over the lectern. With his beard, the twenty-five-year-old looked very serious and definitely older. König later recalled:

> This lecture was a great success. I spoke to about one thousand people in the *Schreinerei* (the carpentry workshop) which was still being used as an improvised lecture hall … As a result of this lecture, numerous invitations came my way to hold lectures at different cities in Switzerland and Germany.[30]

In a letter dated January 5, 1928, to Joseph Emanuel Jan van Leer, a Dutch anthroposophist living in Vienna who had probably recommended Karl König to her, Ita Wegman wrote:

> Dr König outshone himself and kept the whole room in breathless suspense during the entire talk. It was an extraordinarily meaningful lecture. I myself, who only gave him the opportunity to speak on trust and was therefore somewhat worried, because I could not know in advance how the lecture would succeed – although I knew the content beforehand – was extremely surprised and pleased about the great success. So your advice was very good, which prompted me to call this young man to come here.[31]

After his first lecture, König was invited to Basel, Stuttgart, Jena, Leipzig, Breslau (today Wrocław in Poland) and Berlin. In Jena he was given the opportunity to visit the Lauenstein care home. The institute based its work on Rudolf Steiner's curative education course and it was for the children in its care whom Steiner had originally given much of his curative educational and medical advice.[32]

During this period, König had frequent opportunities to discuss his experiences with Tilla Maasberg, and Tilla told him about the small curative educational home she had established with her sister Maria close to their home. They had since been joined in this endeavour by Albrecht Strohschein, one of the group of people who had approached Steiner to give the course in curative education. Strohschein had come to Breslau in 1927 and had agreed in consultation with Ita Wegman to help Tilla and Maria Maasberg set up the curative home. Shortly after Christmas, however, Tilla had to return home to care for her seriously ill sister, Lene. Tilla asked König if he would visit them in Gnadenfrei and examine Lene. It would also give him the chance to see the curative home at the *Waldhaus*. This visit became possible a few months later when König was invited to Breslau to give lectures.

König had given a series of lectures in Dornach in March 1928 at the invitation of the Youth Section at the Goetheanum. In an exchange of letters with Norbert Glas, Ita Wegman expressed her wish that König should 'be able to work mainly scientifically and to be free to lecture'.[33]

The overall response to König's lectures during these months was very positive. This changed on May 28, 1928, when he gave the lecture 'The Embryological Sheathes As an Expression of the Logos: The Archetype of the Human Being':

> On Whitmonday I was asked to give another lecture at the *Schreinerei* in Dornach. The young 'upstart', however, met the strong opposition of a group of people who wanted to make his life difficult within the Anthroposophical Society.[34]

This was a group predominantly centred around Marie Steiner, who, it seems, reacted with indignation to this lecture.[35]

3
The Years in Silesia (1928–35)

The *Waldhaus*

In the early summer of 1928, Karl König went on a lecture tour of various cities. During his stay in Breslau he visited Tilla Maasberg in Gnadenfrei. He later described the deep impression the visit made on him:

> An extraordinary event awaited me at Gnadenfrei – an experience that rooted itself in the depths of my soul and became a formative influence on my further destiny. What I encountered there was not yet known to me, but even so, strings began to vibrate within me, drawing out melodies which had never before resounded in my inner world. At that time Gnadenfrei was still a small village; a self-contained island … It still had much of its original character, probably still from the time when it was first established in the mid-eighteenth century. It was typical of the settlements built by the Herrnhuter, a brotherhood originally founded by Count Zinzendorf. At the large square there were two mighty residential buildings, one for the brothers and another for the sisters. There was also a church – its interior still bright, refined and

The Waldhaus, *the former holiday residence of the Maasberg family, was established as a curative educational home by Tilla and Maria Maasberg.*

quiet. I was deeply moved by the simple, solemn atmosphere that filled this space. 'The Table of the Lord' was positioned higher than the rows of congregation benches. It was surrounded by a gallery and the high windows brought bright light flooding into this true House of God. 'How beautiful,' I thought to myself, and I was filled with a great joy. God's acre – the cemetery – lay behind the village and was surrounded by tall trees. Broad pathways led to the graves: each had a headstone; none was any larger than the other. Everyone is equal in death! Here too an earnest and dignified mood reigned; there was no evidence of pomp and pageantry. 'Yes,' I thought, 'this is the way that life and death should be carried in a community of human beings.' The encounter was graced and I was filled with joyful amazement when I realised the significance of this event. Rarely had a place and its atmosphere affected me so directly.'[1]

Meeting Tilla's family was also enjoyable, as König went on to describe:

> Tilla Maasberg's family received me warmly. I visited her sister Lene, spoke to her parents and then we travelled up to the *Waldhaus* where Mr Strohschein and Maria Maasberg welcomed me. I also met the children and felt immediately at home with them. The next day was Ascension. Following a morning celebration together with the children we went on a tour of the children's home and the beautiful park. We spoke a great deal about curative educational work and I was asked if I would be prepared to work there as a doctor. I expressed my willingness, but said that a larger house would have to be found in order to generate enough work.[2]

Pilgramshain

Only a few hours later the situation changed with the arrival of Joachim and Dorothea von Jeetze. The couple owned a large estate close to the small town of Striegau where they were experimenting with the new biodynamic method. This holistic approach to agriculture had arisen out of the Agricultural Course given by Rudolf Steiner in Koberwitz in 1924, which the von Jeetzes had attended.[3] The couple, however, were in difficulty:

> They could no longer afford to maintain the estate and had come to ask Mr Strohschein if he would take on the Pilgramshain Castle and its estate. They were willing to make these buildings and grounds available for curative educational work.[4]

Pilgramshain, where Karl König established a care home for children and young people with developmental difficulties.

Under these new circumstances, Karl König was happy to cooperate as medical director and promised to start work at the beginning of September. His growing affection for Tilla Maasberg also played an important role:

> On this very day, my dormant love for Fräulein Maasberg opened its wings and found faint approval. All this was still very tender and a subtle awakening process. We hardly exchanged a word about this turn in our friendship, but somewhere deep in our hearts, we knew our common destiny.[5]

Although Ita Wegman had hoped for König's help in setting up her clinic in Arlesheim, she supported him in his new tasks in the following years as best she could.[6] In the summer of 1928, König accompanied Ita Wegman first to Holland to found a clinic and then to London for the World Conference on Anthroposophy. There he met various personalities from the anthroposophical movement and formed lifelong friendships with several of them. For König it was also his first encounter with the English language and the culture of the British Empire.

At the beginning of September 1928, Karl König travelled to Silesia and was picked up by Tilla Maasberg at Striegau railway station.[7] Pilgramshain Castle had to be renovated and made suitable for the children's needs. The funds were limited, everyone had to lend a hand.

During these first weeks, Bertha König visited her son to care for him during an illness, and there she also had her first direct experience of the rising National Socialism and antisemitism in Germany:

> This all happened on the day that Hitler held his first rally in Breslau … Hundreds of people streamed into the hall, all with expectant faces. One man spoke to me and asked why I was not going in with the others for this was our saviour who was going to speak … I told my husband about the situation … and this greatly depressed us.[8]

Soon a large group of children in need of special care arrived. Various Berlin youth welfare offices sent adolescents with developmental difficulties to Pilgramshain, so that within a short time eighty children and youngsters were being cared for in the large castle. After two years the number had risen to one hundred. It was a great challenge to meet the many different needs and demands. The school management was in the hands of Albrecht Strohschein. As medical director, König was able to expand his knowledge of child development disorders and their curative and therapeutic treatment. He was soon very busy with his medical practice on site, to which patients came from all over Silesia, and with his extensive lecturing activities, which often took place outside Pilgramshain.

Karl König at his desk in Pilgramshain.

Marriage and family life

A few weeks later, Karl König proposed to Mathilde Maasberg. He warned her that it would not be easy to be married to him, he was a man dedicated to a purpose, but this did not deter her.[9] They were married on May 5, 1929, by Emil Bock, one of the founding priests of The Christian Community. According to the available documents, König, despite his mother's account, only officially resigned from the Jewish religious community in Vienna in April 1929 shortly before the wedding.[10] It was not until 1937 that he was baptised into The Christian Community in Vienna by the Czech priest Josef Král.[11]

Bertha König wrote about her son's wedding:

> The wedding ceremony was very strange for us ... We got to know the Licentiate Priest Emil Bock ... I remained for a further day. I had a look around and saw everything was progressing. In the meantime, my son had now acquired a small new house. I came away feeling satisfied. My son and daughter-in-law visited us during their honeymoon. They did not stay with us but simply came (for meals). And so we came to know our daughter-in-law better. She was a very fine person, very quiet; if a little melancholic.[12]

Bertha König saw her son more often during this period. König was increasingly busy in Bohemia and Prague, which presented him with more opportunities to visit Vienna, and Bertha visited Pilgramshain regularly.[13] It was there that she met the Rascher family, whom she knew from Vienna. Ilse Rascher had met Karl König at an anthroposophical study group when she was fifteen, and after marrying Michael Rascher she joined in with the work at Pilgramshain, full of idealism. Bertha König's ambivalence about the whole

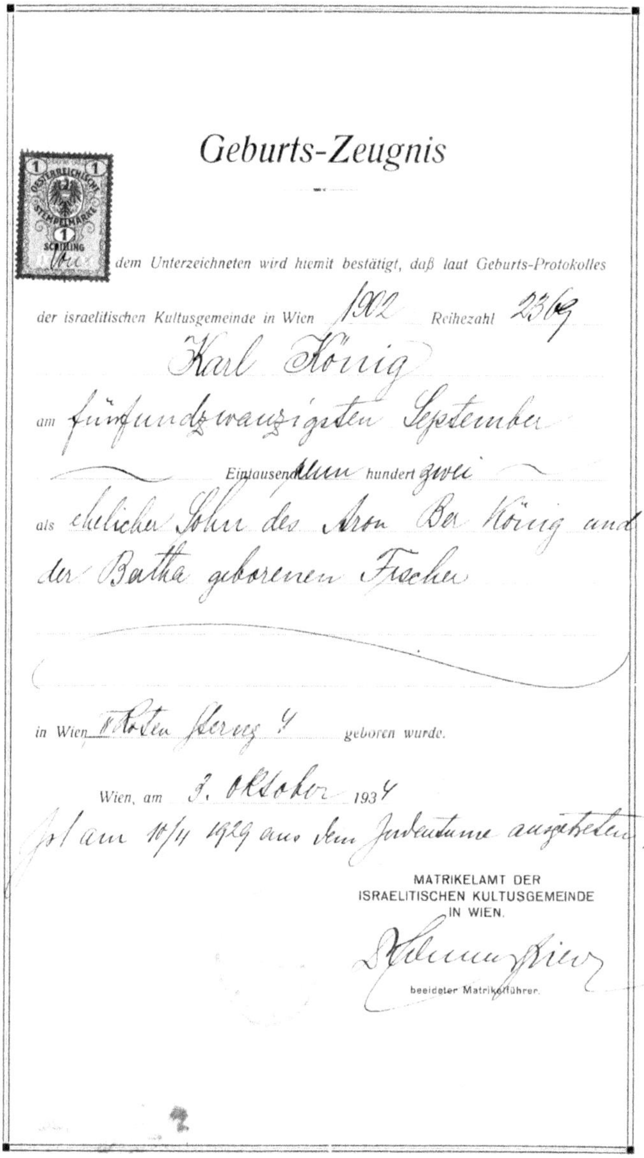

Geburts-Zeugnis

Von dem Unterzeichneten wird hiemit bestätigt, daß laut Geburts-Protokolles der israelitischen Kultusgemeinde in Wien 1902 Reihezahl 2369

Karl König

am fünfundzwanzigsten September

Eintausendneun hundert zwei

als ehelicher Sohn des Aron Ber König und der Batha geborenen Fischer

in Wien II Roten Sterng. 4 geboren wurde.

Wien, am 3. Oktober 1934

Ist am 10/4 1929 aus dem Judentume ausgetreten.

MATRIKELAMT DER
ISRAELITISCHEN KULTUSGEMEINDE
IN WIEN.

beeideter Matrikelführer.

Karl König's birth certificate identifying him as a member of the Jewish religious community in Vienna. At the bottom is a declaration of his withdrawal on April 10, 1929.

enterprise is made clear by her later description of this situation:

> I went to the Raschers', a family we had known in Vienna, who were already married and with whom I was very friendly. I asked Mr Rascher if he had given up a good job and he agreed that was the case. He had been employed as a senior official in an Electricity Works in Vienna and he told me the following story. He had spoken with the Director of the Electricity Works and told him that he was giving up his job. The Director asked if he wanted a higher salary, but Mr Rascher indicated that he was not interested in a higher salary, indeed he did not want a salary at all. The Director replied in good Viennese that he must be crazy and held his head in his hands. He thought there was something not quite right and I was beginning to have the same thought.[14]

Bertha followed the life of her son and daughter-in-law, and supported the family during their financial bottlenecks as well as she could. She also followed the development at Pilgramshain, as she described:

> The castle was rebuilt inside and the grounds were expanded to accommodate the many friends who had come to learn and help. They participated in all the work … including agriculture. They were all responsible for a certain number of children because that was all part of the process of caring. There were teachers and doctors who were still studying, engineers … all of whom had come to participate in this wonderful work and of course without payment, except for their keep. They carried out all

> the work, cooking, washing dishes and helping the children.[15]

It wasn't long before Karl and Tilla were expecting their first child. Bertha recorded the moment in her memoir:

> Our grandchild came into the world on the 3rd December, 1930 and was given the name Renate Clara. I went to the christening and Mr Bock, the priest who married my children,[16] also christened our small Renate. I bought a very beautiful pram with all the necessary bits and pieces. I was very pleased with it. The small house in which my children lived was very well appointed; there was a small front garden and behind a vegetable garden. The house consisted of a small apartment on the ground floor and a slightly bigger one on the first floor. There was a beautiful living-room that was later used as a nursery: it was large enough to meet the needs of the two other children that were to follow ... We had two more grandchildren, Christof (Christoph) and Andreas, who were born in the period 1930–1935 . [Later in Vienna] the fourth grandchild Veronika [was born].[17]

After the birth of her first child, Tilla König devoted herself entirely to her family. Their son Christoph later recalled that his mother was the main caregiver for the children, and that bedtimes were a particularly intimate occasion, with a prayer written by their father for each child and one for the whole family.[18]

During this time, König's medical work increased as he received a regular stream of patients from all over Silesia. Sometimes, when there were too many visitors and strangers in Pilgramshain, Tilla's shyness got the better of

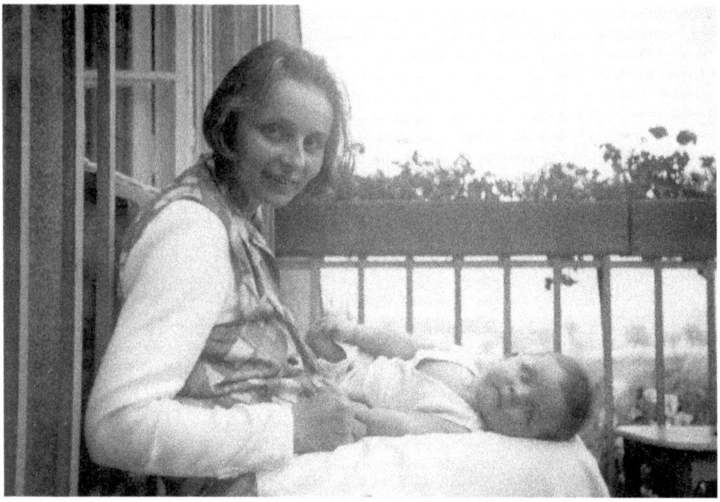

Tilla König with her daughter Renate Clara.

her and she ran away and hid in the woods. König would run after her until he found her and brought her back.

Every fortnight Karl König visited Prague, which, since 1918, had been the capital of the newly founded Czechoslovakia. There he held regular consultations for patients and organised intensive medical work meetings with several Czech doctors.[19]

Ita Wegman as a mentor

During these years, König hardly had any time for his own more extensive studies and research. He did, however, maintain a close relationship with Ita Wegman, who regularly invited him to Arlesheim to lecture and visited him several times in Pilgramshain. She was godmother to his eldest daughter, Renate.[20]

As head of the Medical Section of the School of Spiritual Science at the Goetheanum, Ita Wegman maintained a lively

Karl König reading to Christoph and Renate.

exchange with professionals from the fields of medicine, pharmacology, nursing, curative education and the various therapeutic fields that emerged during this period. Her network extended throughout France and Holland all the way to England, where she cultivated contacts and friendships in influential circles. She organised training and further education courses from 1925 onwards.

It was precisely in the practical and organisational field that she achieved extraordinary things, not only in medical work and curative education, but also in distributing medicines through Weleda and in organising fundraising. Karl König regarded Ita Wegman as a leader in this role throughout her life. She was in close contact with the priests of The Christian Community, with whom she was linked through their joint pastoral-medical work. At the same time, she was the one who worked to ensure that the non-denominational Christian services originating from Waldorf schools' free religion lessons were also established in the context of curative education.[21]

The Nurses' Course held in Arlesheim, with Karl König and Ita Wegman standing on the left at the end of the middle row.

Ita Wegman appreciated König's medical and scientific abilities, but she quickly realised that he needed her support and close guidance, whilst also leaving him free to advance his work in an appropriate manner. She was a staunch supporter of König from the beginning: already at the start of their acquaintance she gave him important lecture assignments for the Medical Section, supporting him on his sometimes difficult path within the Anthroposophical Society and the curative educational movement. In many conversations with other anthroposophists she interceded on his behalf.[22]

The Free School for Social Work

König's social conscience, which had shown itself during his student days through his interest in socialism, increasingly led him to the belief that religion and art should contribute more towards healing society. It was this belief that prompted him to become involved in a series of pastoral-medical courses in collaboration with Emil Bock and The Christian Community between 1929 and 1932.

As early as the spring of 1929, the Central Welfare Office (an umbrella organisation that coordinated private and public welfare organisations) had approached The Christian Community in Berlin to help with probationary assistance for young offenders; something similar happened in Hamburg. At around the same time, the directors of the welfare school in Eisenach sought to orientate their various educational courses towards the more holistic conception of the human being described by anthroposophy. Welfare schools were specialised professional institutions that were established to train social workers, teachers and educators, and healthcare providers. From the beginning of the 1930s the school in Eisenach was in contact with the pastoral medical work of *Allgemeine Soziale Hilfe* [general social assistance], founded by Ita Wegman in connection with the Medical Section at the Goetheanum. Anthroposophically oriented physicians were particularly involved in this as were priests of The Christian Community. In Wuppertal-Barmen in Germany, priest Hilmar von Hinüber established a programme of intensive pastoral care for prisoners and ex-offenders, and his colleague Carl Stegmann had founded the School for Workers in Essen.

The courses were held mostly in those areas where the first urban congregations of The Christian Community had formed and were attended by people from the various fields of social work. This led to an intensive professional cooperation between Karl König and Emil Bock, and the two became good friends from this point on.

Emil Bock reported on one such course with König on December 21, 1929:

> The course was well prepared … About 200 participants attended for three days, half of whom were outside welfare and social workers … Working together with König is always something happy [and the] joint consultation hours we held as doctor and priest, where we were able to see at least some of the 'cases' to be discussed, were also very helpful … I think there will be something like that in the future, where doctors and priests can be consulted together. The presence of the doctor gives authority to the conversation, the presence of the priest gives it spiritual openness. There are millions of borderline cases between the medical and the pastoral.[23]

König always made sure that Ita Wegman was informed about the topics to be covered. Political issues and issues relevant to current social work were addressed at these courses, from unemployment, violence and crime, to suicide, sterilisation and eugenics. They also dealt with issues relating to sex and sexuality, including prostitution, homosexuality and abortion.

In response to the programme of a similar conference in Hanover, a highly critical article appeared, anonymously, in the Newsletter of the Anthroposophical Society on January 25, 1931. The article's author believed that such courses and conferences endangered the strict, spiritual purity of anthroposophy. The following issue of the newsletter, published a few weeks later on February 15, included a defence of the Hanover conference by a participant followed by an extremely critical and negative reply by Marie Steiner, Rudolf Steiner's widow and executor of his estate. In view of König's young age, Marie Steiner believed he was not capable of speaking about such things in an appropriate manner.[24]

Just as the content of these courses caused uproar, so did

Emil Bock (left) with Karl König in Eisenach in 1932.

the criticism that was published in the Anthroposophical Society's newsletter, some of which related to Karl Konig as a person. Despite this, there was some positive feedback.[25]

Emil Bock, who participated in this work with König, made a statement to his colleagues on March 31, 1931, about the courses, including the one in Hanover that had triggered so much criticism. He also referred to the criticism of König, which seems to have been widespread:

> I can say that I look back on these events with joy. They have certainly achieved a lot for the anthroposophical movement as a whole and also for our congregations. The Hamburg event in particular was a great success ... But I must say that it has always given me great pleasure and satisfaction to work with Dr König. As far as the wording of topics ... is concerned, one can be careful to avoid mistakes in the future. But regarding the content, I can say with a clear conscience: everything was fine and of a well-acceptable standard. I say this especially with regard to Dr König ... There he spoke in a really beautiful and human way [with] precision and out of practical experience ... In the first joint course two years ago in Berlin, it was still the case that softness took up too much space with König. He often struck religious notes and I had to try to add the anthroposophical content. But that soon got better, and perhaps we both learned a great deal by working together to find the specific methods.[26]

This work culminated at Whitsun 1932 when König helped to found the Free School for Social Work at Eisenach, for which the already existing welfare school had laid the foundations. At the school's opening, Emil Bock, who had been tasked with its spiritual guidance, spoke about the Sermon on the Mount. He described it as shaping both the content and the goal of care. His colleague Gertrud Spörri addressed the social position of women, and Hilmar von Hinüber spoke on welfare and the human being. König, as a doctor, added a medical perspective on the anthroposophical study of the human being. Forty participants out of one hundred who attended the opening remained for the subsequent two-week inaugural course.

Hitler's seizure of power less than a year later at the end of January 1933 put an end to this pastoral-medical social impulse. Soon all welfare work would be standardised in line with National Socialist ideology.[27]

Political upheavals and exclusion from the Anthroposophical Society

The political situation changed dramatically in 1933 when Hitler and the National Socialists came to power. Bertha König described the impact this had on life at Pilgramshain:

> [Hitler] could not tolerate crippled or mentally retarded children [and] concern for the lives of the children at Pilgramshain intensified day by day. Commissions came and inspected everything … The situation in Pilgramshain became increasingly threatening … because my son [as medical director] was a Jew.[28]

It became clear that Nazi rule in Germany threatened many people, among them people like Karl König, who had a Jewish background, but also all children and adults with any kind of infirmity or disability. As early as July 1933 the

Law for the Prevention of Hereditary Sick Offspring was passed.[29] Unfortunately, the anthroposophical institutions in Germany did not pursue a unified strategy in their confrontation with National Socialism, and in some cases were not at all prepared for what they faced.[30]

The astute and politically aware Ita Wegman, however, was in constant conversation with a number of people from well-informed circles.[31] Already in January 1933 she discussed necessary protective measures and a possible resistance strategy with Karl König, and in a letter dated April 28, 1933, she expressed her concerns about the intensifying threat from the Nazi regime to the Dutch psychiatrist Willem Zeylmans van Emmichoven. Six weeks later, Ita Wegman received a report from her economic assistant, Erich Kirchener, who said the following about Karl König:

> In Pilgramshain there are numerous intrigues targeting Dr König and aiming at his deportation because of his Jewish and foreign origin. Actually, he has already been denied the right to keep his title of Doctor because he obtained his doctor's degree abroad ... Bert Keyserlingk told me that König has said that he would not be able to endure this witch-hunt against him for more than a few weeks and would prefer to leave. He called off a lecture in a neighbouring town because prior to this he had been told by the National Socialist side that the lecture would be disrupted in the middle ... and that he would be prevented from continuing. Even if in the current situation, and with the contacts which can be made to the present government authorities in Silesia, König's continuance could perhaps be forced through, I still think that his activities will not be of much effect anymore and

> that, apart from this, the Institute would very likely suffer considerably.[32]

At the end of March, König received a visit from Walter Johannes Stein, who was also closely associated with Ita Wegman. Because of the growing differences within the Anthroposophical Society, Stein had decided to emigrate to England and encouraged Karl König to do the same, but the latter was not yet ready.

It was still possible for König to work as a doctor in Bohemia and Austria, which at the time were independent of Germany, and to speak publicly at conferences. Under the protection of anthroposophical institutions he was allowed to practise medicine in Germany despite the withdrawal of his doctorate, and Ita Wegman continued to invite him to give lectures and courses at her clinic in Arlesheim in Switzerland. But here König was increasingly caught in the crossfire of the internal power struggles within the Anthroposophical Society that had arisen after Rudolf Steiner's death in 1925. These reached their climax in 1935 when various important personalities were expelled from the society, among them Ita Wegman and many of those close to her within the Medical Section. These included Karl König, who had already incurred Marie Steiner's displeasure with the talk he gave on embryology in 1928 and then with his statements and activities in the run-up to the founding of the Free School of Social Work in 1932. König's articles in the journal *Natura,* founded by Ita Wegman, had also been heavily criticised by various doctors around Friedrich Husemann, one of the first anthroposophical medical doctors who had worked closely with Rudolf Steiner. In all these disputes König always sided with Ita Wegman and in mid-February 1935 he expressed his position in the weekly journal *Das Goetheanum.* At the General Assembly in April 1935 the expulsions took place.

K ö n i g, Karl Dr. med. ~~[illegible] April 1935~~

gestorben

?62092 27. III. 66.

** UEBERLINGEN 526 Telefon

** ~~Brachenreuthe 526 Telefon~~ AV

Adresse: Schloss Pilgramshain, Striegau Land, (Schlesien) — Datum: 1926

Aberdeen / Schottland

1.4.48: Camphill, Milltimber, Aberdeenshire

Okt.55: Milltimber, Aberdeenshire Scotland Camphill House

Juni 62: Bieldside/Aberdeenshire, Scotland Murtle House

Nov.64 : Heimschule , 777 Brachenreuthe ** bei Ueberlingen (Bodensee)

Tel. Ueberlingen 526

Eintritt: A.G. in Oesterreich No.422 — Nr. 1474

Freie A.G.

Übertritt: Okt.33: freistehend Dornach — 1317

geb. 25.9.1902 in Wien

Bemerkungen: i.Versuchsring (Liste Stegemann)

moniert wegen Mitgliedschaft 5.10.33.

red.bez.à Conto 1933

lt Generalversammlungsbeschluss April 1935 ausgeschl.

siehe Generalvers.1948= ist wieder aufgenommen

Austritt:

Karl König's index card at the Anthroposophical Society. Among the information included is a reference to his expulsion from the society in April 1935, crossed out at the top.

Ita Wegman was also excluded from the Executive Council of the General Anthroposophical Society and removed from the leadership of the Medical Section.[33]

In German Silesia, König was still afforded a certain protection since his wife did not have a Jewish background. In 1934, a Whitsun conference with an artistic-therapeutic content took place in Pilgramshain, and there were other opportunities for König to remain publicly active carrying out anthroposophical activities that were still permitted in venues that still allowed them. However, when the support of the Anthroposophical Society fell away, König became more of an undesirable person. Ita Wegman, who continued to influence large sections of the anthroposophic medical profession, including the anthroposophic medicine company, Weleda, lobbied for his support. In Prague in particular, she called on the doctors and representatives of Weleda in May 1935 to publicly stand up for König after a campaign that had damaged his reputation.[34]

After the Nuremberg Race Laws were introduced on September 15, 1935, it became virtually impossible for König to continue working in Germany. He realised that he would have to leave Pilgramshain. In addition, on December 1, 1935, the Anthroposophical Society was banned in Germany and the creation of any successor organisations was forbidden.[35] Correspondence was monitored and at least one of König's letters ended up with the Gestapo.[36]

Another reason König decided to leave, a decision he took together with his wife, was because of the disappointments he had experienced in Pilgramshain and in cooperation with the larger curative education movement in Germany. He expressed this to all concerned in a farewell letter dated February 27, 1936. In it, he justified his departure on the grounds of the lack of support he had received for his perilous situation as a Jew, the lack of will he had encountered in trying to build a community, the unsatisfactory financial arrangements of the staff, and the recurring quarrels and strife.[37]

According to his files, König had treated almost 40,000 patients in the seven years from 1929 to 1936, some of whom had travelled from far away. He was a much sought-after and valued doctor. Bertha König once said of her son that he 'had the ability to read the state of someone's soul from their facial features'.[38] Indeed, many patients later mentioned the special way he treated them, and how he could look at them seriously and yet lovingly. Through conversation and examination he seemed able to get a very comprehensive picture of his patients and then often experienced an inspiration or intuition for future treatment. This must have happened time and again because his name became known and as a result patients came from all walks of life – although the many visiting patients did impair the normal running of the home and contributed to the difficulties König experienced there.

In the heart of Central Europe

At the beginning of March, 1936, Karl and Tilla König and their three children left Silesia for Bohemia near Karlstein Castle, where they spent the spring in the country house of a friend. As newlyweds, the Königs had spent part of their honeymoon in this area seven years earlier.

König was strongly influenced by his home city of Vienna. However, he also felt connected to Silesia and especially to Bohemia with its capital, Prague, which was on the way from Pilgramshain to Vienna. He felt this region to be the heart of Central Europe. His mother's family had lived in Iglau (now Jihlava in the Czech Republic) in the neighbourhood of the family of Gustav Mahler, the composer and conductor he so admired.[39] In an essay on Mahler's life, König wrote:

> The impression of the far-stretching Bohemian-Moravian plains strongly influenced his childhood: the broad and fertile fields of grain, the hills so characteristic of that region, here and there dark forests, brooks and rivers. The land had been permeated by the warm faith of the Bohemian-Moravian Brethren, who had lived and worked there for centuries.[40]

König was particularly fascinated by Karlstein Castle near Prague, which had been built by Emperor Charles IV in 1348. As Emperor of the Holy Roman Empire of the German Nation, he had made Prague the capital and Bohemia the heart of Central Europe. He enforced urban improvements and new administrative structures between secular and ecclesiastical powers. König described how this also manifested architecturally at Karlstein Castle in his short story 'The Three Days':

> The castle was built in a threefold way. Down below are all the rooms serving daily life – the servants' quarters, kitchen and cellar, stalls and stores. But higher up there are those rooms, which do not serve the needs of the body, but the needs of the soul. There is the chapel and there are the rooms in which music was played and sculptures were put on display, all things belonging to the joys and sorrows of the soul. And above these, at the very top … there is a single chamber and this serves the needs of the spirit … The emperor … used to come here every year before Easter. From the evening of Maundy Thursday until the morning of

> Easter Sunday he would lock himself into the little room … Sparse food and urgent documents would be pushed through the little hole in the floor … and no one was allowed to call him. During these days of Passiontide he remained deep in prayer and meditation and in this way he would find strength for the heavy burden of his office.[41]

Under the alias of 'Markus',[42] König described the immediate effect the castle had on himself:

> But for Markus it was an especially deep experience: from that moment onwards this little chamber remained engraved in his soul and, in difficult times and significant moments later in life, he rarely forgot to remind himself of this sight. From that time onwards he tried, in the time before Easter, to have a quiet hour for himself during the day, in order to strive for what this emperor had once attempted to live through as an example for others.[43]

The personality of Duke Albrecht von Wallenstein, general and politician in the Thirty Years' War (1618–48), also impressed König. As a general of an army committed to the emperor in Vienna, Wallenstein was nevertheless a very independent personality. He had been involved with peace negotiations with the opposing Protestant side early on. As ruler of a small duchy in northern Bohemia at the confluence of the rivers Eger and Elbe, Wallenstein had tried to create a country in which all people could live happily and in peace, what he called 'Friedland' ('land of peace') or 'Terra Felix' ('happy land' or 'fortunate land'). He built towns for his subjects with hospitals for the sick, the poor and orphans. He wanted a clear separation of jurisdiction and administration, where trade and commerce could flourish, enabling the development of cultural life. Friedland was autonomous and troops were not permitted to pass through. However, halfway through the Thirty Years' War, Wallenstein was assassinated and his Duchy of Friedland dissolved.[44]

But the ideal of Friedland or Terra Felix, a happy land, remained. Both Charles IV's ideas and Wallenstein's Friedland impulse were to inspire Karl König in his search for appropriate forms of community for his future task. He saw in both endeavours the first beginnings of a threefold social order in which the cultural, economic and political spheres of life could develop independently of each other.[45]

At the beginning of May 1936, Karl König and his family left Bohemia and moved to Vienna, where they had recently found a new family home.

4
The Viennese Years and Emigration (1936–38)

A new beginning

At the beginning of May 1936, Karl König returned with his family to his native, still-independent Vienna. However, the political atmosphere there had changed. The Social Democrats were no longer in power; instead, the reactionary forces of Austrofascism ran the city.

König and his family had not been allowed to bring any money back with them from Germany and so they were forced to start over again, focussing all their energy on setting up a medical practice. With the help of friends, they were able to move into a residential building at Anastasius-Grün-Gasse 49 in the bourgeois 18th district of Währing.

Sali Gerstler (later known as Barbara Lipsker), whose younger brother, Moritz, had been one of the first children to be cared for at Pilgramshain in 1928, became the König's live-in nanny.[1] When she moved into the family home, she was amazed at the aesthetic lifestyle, which was characterised by a rhythm between bustle and meditative calm:

> I was now able to get to know Dr König much more closely in a quite different situation. The house, 49 Anastasius Grün Street, was bright and friendly. It was furnished simply but tastefully and artistically … The children lived in a very large nursery with a big sunny terrace … The way Mrs König ran her household, her harmonious, even movements, how she dealt with her children, approached her husband, cared for meals, the beauty and order of the house – always with the attitude of devotion in the actual doing. What a lot I had to learn![2]

König's medical practice rooms were located in the same building. König later wrote of this period:

> This was a good training in the practicalities of life and in learning to trust in the spirit. But it was difficult in the beginning. Quite some time passed before the first patients arrived and sometimes I did not know where the money would come from for our daily needs, yet we seldom went hungry … Then, in autumn 1936, a larger number of patients began to visit the practice.[3]

Tilla König helped her husband out in the practice to begin with, but soon she was expecting their fourth child, Veronika, who was born in March 1937.

As the practice expanded, König felt that it was not enough to provide only medical help, and so he started holding a series of weekly lectures in his waiting room for patients.

The future founders

Among the regular attendees of König's weekly lectures was a group of friends, some of whom had known each other since their school days. A few were studying medicine and had met König in 1933 at a medical conference in Arlesheim. Since that time, König had met the entire group during his visits from Pilgramshain. The members of this group would play a significant role in König's work and some of them would go on to found the Camphill Movement with him.

Sali Gerstler described in her memoirs how this group of young people first met Karl König:

> Every Thursday night many of us gathered in the rooms used by The Christian Community … Sometimes I would tell my friends of Dr König and of my brother whom I loved so much. Three of the friends [Hans Schauder, Edi Weissberg and Hanna Förster] were studying medicine and as a result of a growing interest in anthroposophy two of them took part in a conference for medical students in Arlesheim. It was there that they got to know Dr König.[4]

König soon became an important person for the whole group, as Sali went on to describe:

> For us he was the person who made one feel known and appreciated … We asked Dr König to meet our whole group and it was from that time onwards that we had meetings together whenever he came to Vienna. Very frequently he gave lectures in anthroposophical circles or also public lectures, and we would meet afterwards in one of the Viennese

> coffee houses, sitting together for hour after hour to discuss world perception, political questions or very personal questions together ... We could also turn to him as a doctor and receive help. It seemed that our lives gained a new dimension, a new meaning. We endeavoured to recognise the signs of our time and its demands upon us ... Every week one of us brought a leading thought, a verse, a sentence from the Bible, a poem, a significant thought from a book.[5]

The core of this circle of friends was drawn from a class of the Wasa Gymnasium (a secondary school). It consisted of Hans Schauder, Eduard 'Edi' Weissberg (later known as Edward Whitmont), Rudi Lissau and Bronja Hütter. Hans Schauder had already completed an internship with König in Pilgramshain as part of his medical studies,[6] and Edi Weissberg was hired as an assistant in König's practice. Alex Baum made friends with them towards the end of his school days. Bronja brought her friend Elisabeth 'Lisl' Schwalb (later Schauder) into the group, who in turn met Sali Gerstler and Trude Blau (later Amann) through her involvement with the Socialist Workers' Youth. Hans Schauder sat next to Hanna Förster on their first day of medical school, and Hanna later introduced her sister Hedda (later Lissau) to the group. Rudi Lissau's younger sisters Hanna and Susanne (later Müller-Wiedemann) were also part of the circle.[7] Trude Blau and Hanna Lissau, who belonged rather peripherally to the group, received their curative education training at the Sonnenhof in Arlesheim from 1936 onwards.[8]

It was Rudi Lissau who had introduced the friends to anthroposophy; his family had often played host to Rudolf Steiner during the latter's visits to Vienna.[9]

Expansion of the group

After a while a second group of young people, some of whom had known each other for some time, joined König's weekly lectures, which soon had to be held in a public hall because of the growing interest in them. The group included two medical students, Thomas Weihs and Peter Roth, Peter's younger sister Alix, who was a photographer, and art student Carlo Pietzner. They came from the more affluent backgrounds that went hand in hand with a certain carefree lifestyle and an upper-middle-class *savoir vivre,* which meant they knew how to behave in polite society. They were several years younger than the original group that had formed around König. For them, the encounter with anthroposophy was completely new, and this brought a fresh invigoration to the meetings when these two groups united under König's guidance.

König had a formative influence on these younger people, who approached the new ideas with great openness, interest and enthusiasm. A common vision based on König's first experience of the Advent garden came into being:

> During the year 1937, this youth group became a source of great satisfaction to me. I was able to mould a younger generation and lead them step by step to an understanding of the spiritual realities of the world. In the course of this year, it became evident that we ought not only to study together but that we should in time do some common work.[10]

A good basis for working together was found in staging the so-called Oberufer Christmas plays. These are a series of medieval mystery plays – the Paradise Play, the Nativity

Play and the Epiphany Play – that were rediscovered and published in the eighteenth century by the Austrian linguist Karl Julius Schröer, a mentor and friend of Rudolf Steiner. They are named after the Austrian village of Oberufer (part of modern-day Bratislava in Slovakia) where they were discovered.[11] These plays were performed during Christmas 1936 and 1937 in the rooms of the Swedish Israel Mission in Vienna. As a common subject of study, the group also studied the artistic works and biographies of young people who had died in the First World War, among them Bernhard von der Marwitz, Otto Braun, Franz Marc, August Macke and others. This gave rise to questions about destiny and development, which prompted a more in-depth study of lectures by Rudolf Steiner. As König wrote:

> We sensed that these young people had attempted to prepare the ground for something we should continue. Thus we found our way into the stream of historic evolution. We did not want to remain on the fringes of this endeavour, but wished, on the contrary, to be part of making one of Central Europe's tasks become reality.[12]

Together the members of the group read Rudolf Steiner's lectures of the Pedagogical Youth Course, which he had given for young people in 1922.[13] In their discussions they came to the conclusion that a seed of renewal had to be implanted into civilisation. The desire arose in many of them not only to study anthroposophy but to live and work out of it, ideally in community.

During this time, König was in regular contact with his mentor, Ita Wegman, who followed his medical work as well as his social activities. In one letter to him she wrote:

> It was a great joy to me that you have started a youth group which is doing good work, as you write in your letter. That you are successful and will continue to be, dear Dr König, does not surprise me because there is something about Austria, and you feel the same, which is certainly important for promoting spirituality. That Dr Steiner was born and used to live there … is indeed a fact that contributes to the success of spiritual work. The soul-needs and the hardships of everyday life can bring out something which does not arise in life's abundance.[14]

König later described the relationship he had with some members of the Anthroposophical Society in Vienna, from which he had been expelled in 1935:

> During this time, I was not very popular among the strict and dogmatic followers of Rudolf Steiner. I pursued my own way and did many things differently from what they thought right. I had the strong intention to make myself inwardly free from all kinds of sectarianism and to recreate Rudolf Steiner's ideas within myself … I promised myself not to speak about anything for which I could not take full personal responsibility.[15]

The last year in Vienna

The political situation in Austria was becoming increasingly threatening, and antisemitic attacks had intensified in Vienna through the activities of various groups sympathetic to the German National Socialists. With 170,000 Jewish inhabitants, Vienna had the densest settlement of European

Jews.[16] König's mother, Bertha, described her experience of antisemitism when she visited Tilla in the Rudolfinger House hospital after the birth of her daughter, Veronika, in the spring of 1937:

> Already Hitler's power began to be felt. On one occasion [my] son [caught] the chauffeur who was very devoted to the family, wearing an SA uniform. I often used to visit my daughter-in-law at Rudolfinger House and the chauffeur would bring me home and was very polite to me. It was not easy for my children living there when the persecution began. My daughter-in-law was afraid to walk the streets lest she be abused even though she was a Christian. Although all the employees were Christian, many rich Jews lived in this particular district of Vienna. Misfortune soon started.[17]

Some of König's patients came from very influential circles in politics, business, culture and the arts. He was surprised by their attitude towards what was going on:

> I met a great number and variety of people, and I was forced to realise – with confusion and amazement – that even the best-informed were blind to what was actually happening in Central Europe. They all hoped that it 'would not be too bad'.[18]

In the summer of 1937, König spent a ten-day holiday in the southern Bohemian monastery of Hohenfurth, the home of the poet Adalbert Stifter. He also took a steamer trip with his wife along the Danube via Budapest to the Black Sea, where they spent a few days. As on all his journeys, König felt strongly about the new landscape and always tried to understand it in its larger historical context. From this region came the Christian movement of the Bogomils with its Manichaean origins – partly Eastern and influenced by Buddhism – which was considered heretical by the Catholic Church. He must have told Ita Wegman about it, because two years later, in August 1939, she wrote to him in detail about her own summer journey 'to the East', which also took her to the Black Sea.[19]

The following autumn, König's work intensified once again due to a steadily growing influx of patients. A larger hall in the city centre had to be found for his lectures. At the same time, it became apparent that Austria, though still independent, was becoming a pawn in the game being played by Nazi Germany and that no help could be expected from Italy, France or Great Britain. Many Austrians, however, were in favour of a union with Germany, and large sections of Vienna's political and administrative class had been infiltrated by Nazi sympathisers who hoped Hitler would bring improvements to their country. König described the months before the German invasion:

> The general mood, however, had changed completely. Now people were filled with deep-seated resignation. Doom and destruction threatened the one; the other hoped that salvation would come from [Germany]. At that time I treated a large number of 'secret' (Nazi) party members in the police and high office and consequently became aware of much more than I actually wanted to know. I refrained from taking up any opportunities that this situation presented because I did not want to withdraw from the fate that was now inevitably approaching [our] group of young friends.[20]

Ann Nederhoed (later known as Anke Weihs) was a

young dancer who first met Karl König in 1938 as a patient at his medical practice. She suffered from a skin problem that had not disappeared despite numerous treatments by experienced specialists. She later described how other friends were sceptical about whether she should really see this doctor, whose methods were considered unconventional. She later described her visit as follows:

> [The] entrance hall was light, the waiting room in no way suggestive of anything but a certain peace. Cane-covered benches stood around the walls and between them were aquaria containing a great variety of small, unusual fish … The waiting room was packed to capacity with waiting patients … Towards evening my name was called … At the desk in the centre stood a very small man with a large head. He wore a physician's white coat. His eyes were very big and grave. When they rested on you, they did not only see through you, they seemed to create you anew … I think this first grave gaze – Dr König otherwise said little – was the initial step in healing. The medicines that followed were effective because something in the inner situation had begun to change – whereby I felt no onrush of sympathy … for this small doctor – I only felt called up, impersonally, to my better self.[21]

The *Anschluss:* March 11, 1938

On the night of January 25, 1938, there was a display of the aurora borealis, the Northern Lights, that lasted for several hours and was visible throughout Central Europe. To many people it seemed like a harbinger of events to come. König wrote of it:

> For some hours … the mighty aura borealis transformed the entire night sky across Europe into flaming red. This seemed to be a portent pleading with humankind to be conscious and to reflect. But only a few heard the voice calling as the Baptist did: 'Change your ways!'[22]

At the beginning of March, the Austrian chancellor, Kurt Schuschnigg, was called to see Hitler at his retreat in Berchtesgaden in the Bavarian Alps. There he was humiliated and pressured into making major concessions that ultimately amounted to the annexation of Austria by the German Reich. As König wrote:

> Austria fell on March 11, 1938 … The German troops crossed the borders and the government was forced to relinquish power. It was a pitiful and disreputable end.[23]

That evening, the group of young friends met at König's home. They were distraught by the day's events and discussed what to do now. Eventually, they agreed to set off individually from Austria and meet again in a safe place as soon as possible. Then they read the last lecture of the Pedagogical Youth Course, which said, among other things:

> The Age of Michael – he who conquers the dragon – must begin, for the power of the dragon has become great! … What we carry in our heads is lost along the way. What we take into our hearts, however, the heart will safeguard in whatever situations and spheres of action we are placed in.[24]

Karl König described that evening as follows:

> Outside the city was raging; Hitler youth in their white stockings, men in brown uniforms, and screeching women all danced around the dragon. Yet in the midst of this insane commotion a flame had been kindled; a flame that was to forge a sword of peace that could, perhaps, also shine as a small light for future deeds.[25]

Hans Schauder also summarised his impressions of that evening:

> I can still conjure up the complete scene of that time. I will never forget it. The so-called youth group … had agreed to meet at Dr König's that evening. Lisl and I went there by tram and had no idea how fateful that evening would be for us. When we got on the tram, we felt immediately an immensely oppressive and spectral atmosphere … It was full and there were no seats left so we were the only people standing. Everyone stared silently at us. No one said a word. And then we saw that all of them without exception had pinned on a swastika … The familiar and chatty Vienna tram of yesterday had suddenly turned into a foreign and hostile means of transport. The others looked at us in silence and it was quite obvious that they considered the two of us, the only ones without swastikas, as creatures without a future. They showed no aggression whatsoever towards us. But we were alone and excluded by silence. When we arrived at Dr. König's flat he greeted us with the words: 'Do you know that Hitler has invaded?' That evening the group, most of them were Jews, debated what the consequences for us were … The meeting in

> Dr König's flat ended very late. Lisl and I no longer dared to take the tram home … It was a terrible walk. I still remember our awful loneliness on that Vienna night in the empty streets … Later that night my friend Rudi Lissau, who had not come to the meeting, told me on the telephone: 'Hans, I am crossing the frontier tonight, are you coming? They will kill us if we do not leave immediately.' I could not make the decision to leave immediately.[26]

With the *Anschluss* – the annexation of Austria – the threat to the Jewish population became immediately real. Vital decisions had to be made quickly and at short notice. But even if young people were more flexible than their elders, many still needed time to prepare. Although Rudi Lissau fled that first night, for others it did not happen so quickly, as Hans Schauder recalled:

> The two of us [Hans and Lisl] needed time to take our farewells. We were too much attached to Vienna. We anticipated the worst from the Nazis but even then most Viennese Jews adopted a wait-and-see attitude. It was simply inconceivable … that a process which had started two hundred years earlier under Josef II, bringing emancipation and full citizens' rights to Austrian Jews and leading to the assimilation of many of us, myself included, should simply come to an end overnight. A taste of the treatment in store from the Nazis came the next day. The mob had daubed Nazi slogans on Vienna's pavement on the night of the invasion. Viennese Jews were hauled out of their flats by Nazi SA men and forced to clean the pavements with toothbrushes and cloths. Of course, they scrubbed at the mess on their knees for hours without success.

> Lisl and I were spared this humiliation. Some of the Viennese Jews who had been rounded up in this way disappeared into camps even then. I very quickly realised that this was not some temporary repression but that life and limb were in danger. I now knew that the Nazis were capable of anything and understood that the Austria which could protect and save me no longer existed. I had to leave the country immediately.[27]

Threats and persecution

Karl König experienced his own personal crisis in the days that followed:

> I too was seized by the epidemic of panic during these days. I saw how everything I had achieved – a growing seed – was collapsing into nothing around me. But my courageous and loyal wife stood by me and within a few hours I had surmounted this crisis.[28]

Furthermore, he described:

> I was often called out as a doctor during these days to attend to suicide cases amongst my patients … One despairing act followed another, and the 'victors' did everything to intensify fear and confusion. They confiscated homes and publicly ridiculed and degraded people on the streets. The victims' fear was so great that they complied without a word.[29]

König was naturally worried about his parents. They

still lived in Leopoldstadt, which was hit even harder by persecution. His mother described those weeks:

> Even though the house staff had put swastika flags in their windows the situation got worse. Many came seeking advice from my son but at that point in time he could do nothing for them or himself … Daily he would come to see how we were. In the Second District where most Jews lived, the situation was particularly bad.[30]

Karl König's father was also affected by the humiliating street cleaning that was typical in Vienna in those days:

> Our shop being located on a corner was a good target for the mob. All the people who earlier had been friends now became enemies, happy to bestow their inner resentment against every expression of Jewishness … Men were taken from their shops and forced to clean cars or streets in front of howling bystanders. My husband was no exception and each of our Jewish friends had this and still more terrible things to endure.[31]

Although the group of young people surrounding König escaped largely unscathed, some of their accounts give an idea of what happened to them and members of their family. Everyone dealt with it in their own way. Marie Blitz (later Korach), a childhood friend of the Roth family and then a patient of König's, later recalled:

> Austria fell like a rotten fruit in twenty-four hours – without a shot being fired – in Hitler's arms. Life began to be very ugly. I was once stopped in town and made to sweep the pavement of a street

> – I was so furious that I went and bought myself a new hat! We were really saved from worse things![32]

Sali Gerstler spent the weeks after the *Anschluss* either with the König family or in her own family's flat in Leopoldstadt. She never left the house without carrying the New Testament in case she was arrested. Men were particularly at risk. In the various raids it was always younger men who were rounded up for forced labour in the concentration and work camps. Sali Gerstler related this experience:

> These last months in Vienna were a very dark time. Persecutions of the Jews started from the moment Hitler marched into Vienna. Our little shop, the source of our daily bread, was attacked and closed down. Already you saw old men down on their knees scrubbing the stones. Rows and rows of young and older men – people you knew – were marched off – where to? You heard screaming and weeping – loud shouting of 'Heil Hitler!' Then there was a knock at the door – a group of men when I opened. 'Is there any man in your flat?!' 'No,' I answered completely calm and cool. They looked at me suspiciously. I made a gesture like inviting them in – they went. Aba, my brother stood hiding behind the bathroom door. All the male [individuals] from the twenty-three flats of our house were [taken away].[33]

In the following weeks, she witnessed König preparing his final departure from Vienna:

> We met almost every day. Dr König drew the

> outlines of the work our group was going to take on. The East was barred for us, we might go to an island: Cyprus perhaps? We would have to take European heritage, culture with us, work on the land, share our lives with handicapped children. We would do all the work ourselves, receive no pay; farmer, teacher, priest, doctor all would carry the community; our way of life would be simple in Christian brotherhood. We warmed to the idea enthusiastically, connected by an inner will that need not be spoken. Finally, a request for entrance as a group was sent to Ireland, which was turned down. But there was no time to be lost, we had to leave Austria individually as soon as possible, especially the men.[34]

In early summer, many of the young people from the circle of friends left Vienna for various European cities: Paris, Prague, Basel, Zurich, Milan, Zagreb and London. König himself described his situation at the time as follows:

> At that point my influential patients began to be helpful to me and by means of high-level protection I acquired a visa for Switzerland. Initially my wife and our four small children were to move to Gnadenfrei (in Silesia) to stay with relatives until a new home could be found … The torment and misery became noticeably worse in Vienna. The Party and the authorities soon began to pressurise me and I knew that I would have to act quickly if I was to escape the Gestapo's web, vanishing without a trace.[35]

König's wife and children were protected by Tilla's

non-Jewish origin. At the time they were in the process of moving to a new, larger flat in nearby Hasenauerstrasse, but they did not live there long. The furniture and household effects were packed up and sent to Switzerland where they were stored until the family's final place of refuge was known.

Escape

During the summer of 1938, König received help in preparing and carrying out his plans to escape Austria from Lucia de Viti de Marco, a patient who lived in Rome and had become a family friend.[36] Donna Lucia, as König called her, handled many of the formalities, including acquiring an entry permit to Italy for him. Tilla and their four children would stay with König's parents before travelling to Gnadenfrei in Silesia. It soon became clear, however, just how little a visa counted for the new rulers when König attempted to cross the Austrian–Italian border in Tyrol with Donna Lucia on August 14. König's mother described what happened:

> He had shown his passport and entry permit for Italy. A Gestapo [officer] said that he had phoned to Vienna and had been told that [König] had a false permit and so he would not be allowed to continue. My son replied that he was surprised the Gestapo would issue false permits. He was told that Donna Lucia could proceed but he should have to remain. Well, you can appreciate my son's predicament … he was psychologically exhausted after all the dreadful weeks of misery leading to all his friends and acquaintances coming to him for help and advice. What now occurred in the police office may happen

> only once in a hundred years and one must believe here in providence and God's help in an emergency. The doors opened and the chief of the Gestapo came out, an enormous man, paralytically drunk who went up to my son and said: 'Hello, old friend, what's the problem?' My son showed him the passport and asked that it be stamped. His pass was authenticated; he was wished a good journey and was shaken by the hand. The chief of the Gestapo then said: 'When you come back, look me up.' They drove off as fast as they could across the border, still bewildered at that what had happened.[37]

König described the events at the border as 'a miraculous crossing made possible with the help of a drunken SA trooper'.[38]

After his terrible experiences, König spent two weeks recovering in Donna Lucia's country house in Italy before travelling to Switzerland.

König was completely penniless and had only been allowed to export 10 Reichsmarks as a refugee (around $90 or £65 in today's money). He had hoped to find work in Arlesheim and though he was very kindly received by Ita Wegman, the other staff were extremely wary. A collaboration with the Swiss Epileptic Institution in Zurich also fell through.

Meanwhile, Tilla and their four children were with König's parents in Leopoldstadt. Bertha König described these weeks:

> It was not easy for them as their clothes and linen had to be constantly unpacked and repacked. Their stay with us was only temporary as they went on to Gnadenfrei. This was understandable as it would be easier and less dangerous to live there because the

> whole family were Christians. In early September she left with the children and their entire luggage. It was a momentous exodus. We accompanied them to the station with sad hearts, always [wondering] what the future would bring and whether we should see our children again.[39]

Where to?

Ita Wegman had long been concerned about the safety of her colleagues of Jewish origin. She followed international politics closely and came to a clear-sighted judgement about developments in Germany. As Zeylmans van Emmichoven would write: 'Through all her travelling, she was very well informed.'[40] As early as February 1938, when it became clear that Austria would not remain independent for much longer, Ita Wegman hinted in a letter to König that she saw a task for him in France. At the same time, König's friend Eugen Kolisko, who had already emigrated to London, tried to obtain an entry permit for König and his family. A letter from the medical doctor Karl Nunhöfer to Ita Wegman dated April 2, 1938, shows that Kolisko hoped for the help of Ita Wegman's influential English friend Dame Florence Simpson:

> I think Dr Kolisko's plan to bring König and his wife over to England with the help of Dame Florence is very daring.[41]

Ita Wegman supported König during this time, and asked him to teach in her nurses' training school in Arlesheim. She also suggested a future collaboration in the curative education initiative in France, the task she had hinted at in her letter to him in February. Despite the failure of earlier attempts to find a suitable place in Cyprus and Ireland, König nevertheless felt confident and travelled to Paris on September 20. A small curative education home was under construction in the Rue de l'Assomption, and there was also a chateau near Versailles where the French curative educator Vala Bérence had moved with the children in her care.

At Michaelmas, König sent a letter from France to his young friends in Vienna. In it, among other things, he said:

> The friends here are hoping for the establishment of an institute with a farm and will help with this initiative ... There are hundreds of estates around that could be rented at a low price ... They hope that something can be found by February or March ... There is also a plan to create a settlement nearby for Christian non-Aryans.[42]

The combination of curative work and biodynamic farming had already been an important aspect of the social and therapeutic way of life in Pilgramshain. In his letter König encouraged his friends to learn French, but he soon came to the conclusion that France would not be a safe place for them in the long-term either.[43]

Entry permit to the UK

At the same time, Kolisko's efforts were successful, for in mid-October König received a letter from the English Consulate General in Bern informing him that he, as one of fifty Austrian doctors, would be allowed to enter the United Kingdom, study there and then set up as a doctor. König consulted Ita Wegman, who immediately offered to help him. She put him in touch with friends who lived just north of Aberdeen in Scotland and who were willing to help:

> I discussed everything with Dr Wegman and she was of the opinion that I should immediately respond to this helping hand stretched out towards me. Previously she had told me about friends living near to Aberdeen who were prepared to provide assistance to a group of refugees. She considered it vital that curative work should begin in Scotland, thereby fruitfully complementing the work that had already started in England. She also promised to give us as much help as possible.[44]

Once again, König was able to count on his Italian friend, Donna Lucia, who accompanied him on the crossing from Calais to Dover on December 8, 1938, and then on to Victoria Station in London, where he was met by some old friends.

König received a great deal of support from Eugen Kolisko, who published the journal *Modern Mystic* and was in the process of setting up the School for Spiritual Science, an anthroposophical college. In addition to their Viennese origins, the two men shared many common interests, especially in relation to the history of Central Europe, which they deepened further through their many conversations. Kolisko had set up a house in London for refugee friends, which is where König went to stay for a brief time. Some members of the group that had formed around König in Vienna were already in England, as were the parents of Peter and Alix Roth. After only a few days, König, Peter Roth and his father, the engineer Emil Roth, travelled by sleeper train to Aberdeen. They had been invited, on the recommendation of Ita Wegman, by William Theodore and Emily Haughton to the Williamston Estate to discuss a future cooperation.

König was impressed by the silence and beauty of the Scottish landscape, and life on the estate seemed to him like something from another world. The Haughtons were willing to make a nearby old vicarage, known as Kirkton House, available to König and his friends for their work:

> The house itself, however, was quite spacious. It had two large rooms on the ground floor, and several rooms on both the first and second floors. although there was neither electric light nor central heating, and there was only a single, ancient bathroom, it seemed to me a quite suitable, even ideal, house for our beginnings. Finally, another roof! And a garden! Mr Houghton also promised us milk and potatoes as initial assistance. We had here the possibility not only of living together, but also of taking in about ten children. What more could we wish for?[45]

The Haughtons promised to install central heating and organise the necessary renovations. Until the house was finished, they agreed to take in Tilla König and the four children as guests. König immediately asked his wife to get a visa in Breslau and to start the journey to Great Britain as soon as possible. This could be organised for the last days of the year.

König also wrote to Ita Wegman after the visit to the estate. She had been a guest of the Haughtons in Williamston some years before and could well imagine the situation. She reaffirmed his decision and encouraged him to take the British medical exams in order to gain full recognition as a doctor in Britain.[46]

On December 19, König sent out a hopeful Christmas

letter to his young friends who were living in many places:

> It is with a joyful heart and in grateful devotion that I write this Christmas greeting to you all today … For two days ago we all came a great deal closer to our goal, and I feel as if now, just before Christmas, a crack has opened in the door that lets us sense the light of our future … [I feel] that we have found the good 'hosts' who want us, and that all our efforts must now be directed towards ensuring that the Word of the World can reveal itself in the work of our hands, in the will of our hearts and in the brightness of our thoughts, but always in the community of our actions.[47]

Christmas in London

Karl König spent Christmas alone and hoped very much that his family's departure would go smoothly; he had not seen them since his sudden flight from Vienna at the beginning of August.

But what could König do to feel united with them at Christmas? He decided to write a Christmas play for his family, in which everyone, even the young children, could play along. With the help of this play, he wished them hope and strength for the difficult times that lay ahead for them all. Thus, the angel, written for the eldest daughter, speaks at the beginning:

> All shining stars bring joy and fun,
> Deep in our hearts awakes the Sun.
> And with all distances in sight
> Day is changing into night.[48]

Many years later, he remembered this Christmas, which

he spent alone in exile in London, in a country still foreign to him, worrying about the uncertain future by the light of a small candle:

> [It] is now twenty-one years ago that I first celebrated this festival here in Britain and not in my own country. I was sitting in a tiny room, in one of the hundreds of back streets of London – alone, a drop in that human sea of a city, a stranger, a foreigner. I knew that together with me, tens of thousands of people shared the same fate … How would we survive?
> The small candle in front of me lit the few green branches and the gas fire hummed a low song. My thoughts went out into the future. Would it be possible to turn this lonely life into order and shape again? … [This] was a country of the Western world. The language was foreign to me; the people were strangers; their way of living was not my way, and their past was almost unknown to me. I had a different background, different modes of existence, different thoughts … I was alone! Would I again have the strength to begin anew? In a few days my wife and children were to arrive, and in several countries of the Continent a number of young friends were waiting to join me. Join me in what? … A house had been found in the north of Scotland, where we could start to live together, but what kind of life would we live? It would only be an enclave in this land; we would be strangers in a big community. And what was our task to be? The light of the candle was now quiet and bright and my eyes turned to a small book that a kind person had given me as a Christmas present.[49]

The 'small book' was a translation of the King James

Bible. The dedication spoke about going forward with the determination to spread the truth of Christ. Inspired by this, the necessity of his emigration began to take on a new meaning in a broader European context:

> Is this not a common ground on which I may stand? I asked myself ... And now I saw and knew more about the future task that lay before me. I saw Austria overrun and conquered by men who had betrayed the very essence of the destiny of Europe. They had turned it into a camp of nationalists, searching for might and power. Europe was overcome by their vain glory and was preparing to become a battlefield. Could we not take a morsel of the true European destiny and make it into a seed so that some of its real task might be preserved: a piece of its humanity, of its inner freedom, of its longing for peace, of its dignity? If this were possible, would it not be worthwhile to live and work again? Let us begin to become a morsel of this Europe which, at the moment, has to disappear. But let us not do it in words but in deeds, to serve and not to rule, to help and not to force; to love and not to harm. This would be our task.[50]

On December 30, 1938, König was able to meet his wife and children at the port of Harwich.[51] A few days later he accompanied them to Williamston in Scotland, where he left them, to begin with, in the care of the Haughtons in their large country house.

Karl König's parents also managed to escape from Vienna. Bertha König described in her memoir how she and her husband, against their son's advice, tried to cross into Croatia illegally at the beginning of March 1939 and ended up in detention. König managed to get them a residence permit for Great Britain, and they were released and finally able to leave for England in May 1939. They lived near Oxford for a few months, then later moved to Aberdeen.[52]

5
Arrival in Scotland (1938–40)

Essential preparations

A few days after taking his family to Williamston in Scotland, Karl König returned to London to take care of the necessary formalities for setting up what would become the curative education community at Kirkton House. Applications for funding were made to the British Home Office, to the Quakers, who at that time were particularly committed to the cause of Jewish refugees,[1] to the Anthroposophical Society and to the Refugee Committee of the Church of Scotland, which then provided a loan.

Following an interview with the relevant Scottish authority in February 1939, two months after his arrival in London, König noted:

> Two months later I was sitting in Edinburgh
> opposite the secretary of the Board of Control;
> that is the authority to which curative education
> institutes are subordinated, and I tried to present my
> plan to him in bad English ... As I spoke, I thought:
> The man will soon point out to me with a smile that
> the door is at my right hand side ... but then he said

> something else: 'For ten years we have been waiting for someone who wants to open a private institute for retarded children; try it.'[2]

The next step was to obtain an entry permit for those members of the Viennese circle of friends who had not already reached Britain by other means. After crucial discussions in mid-March 1939, a General Permit arrived for the whole group, which also allowed them to stay and work on the planned project at Kirkton House. Such a group visa was quite exceptional. It was certainly helpful that Cecil Harwood, the chairman of the Anthroposophical Society in Great Britain, knew the then British Home Secretary, Sir Samuel Hoare, from his student days at Oxford.[3]

König was given the opportunity to study in Dundee at the medical faculty of the University of St Andrews so that he could then obtain his medical licence in the United Kingdom.[4]

Staff would also be needed who were professionally qualified for this work, or who at least brought enthusiasm and openness to furthering their personal, social and curative educational training according to the demands of the community.

The founding members

By the end of 1938, several young people from the Vienna group were already in London. Peter Roth, whom the Nazis had prevented from completing his medical studies in Vienna, had left the city that summer with Ann Nederhoed (later Anke Weihs) and married her in London in August 1938. Ann had spent her childhood in Australia, Japan, the USA and Europe and had trained as a professional dancer.

She was the only one in the group who spoke English as her mother tongue.

Lisl Schwalb (later Schauder) had met the Haughtons at Ita Wegman's clinic in Arlesheim and had been invited by them to Williamston, where she had been living since October 1938, even before Karl König's first visit. Sali Gerstler had received a visa for England in December 1938 to work as a nanny, which she was obliged to do for a year. This meant she was only able to join the community in Scotland at the end of 1939.

At the beginning of 1939, König's former patient Marie Blitz emigrated to England. Although she was already well advanced in her medical studies, as a Jew she had been excluded from studying medicine in Vienna. In London, she worked as an auxiliary nurse in the King Edward VIII Hospital in Ealing. According to her diary entries, she met König five times between January and March 1939, and he invited her to join the founding group at Kirkton House.[5]

Alix Roth, Peter Roth's younger sister, had also managed to flee via Zagreb to London in January 1939, to join her brother and parents who were already there.

Carlo Pietzner, a graduate of the Vienna Art Academy, fled first to Prague to avoid military service in the German Wehrmacht, then to London via Switzerland. Before joining König and the founding group in Scotland, however, he spent some time in the English Lake District

The General Permit also made it possible for other young people with a Jewish background who came from the wider circle of the Vienna group to take refuge in the United Kingdom. Some of those eligible for the collective visa continued their qualification process with Ita Wegman, with whom König maintained a regular correspondence, and she offered them as much protection as possible. In a letter dated August 19, 1939, she wrote to König about some difficulties with the authorities:

> Regarding Miss Lissau we have done the following.[6] When her residence permit came to an end and her situation became desperate we did everything to help her extend it. She has not yet completed her training, especially in music which is her main field. So we offered the authorities a guarantee of 3,000 Swiss francs to keep her here, and this, we have been told, will probably be approved ... Mr Schauder, as you probably know, became ill again, he is in Ascona and I believe already getting better. He is frail, but will possibly be healthier when he can live in a more settled situation and without worry about his future and when the separation from Ms Schwab is also over. Mr Amann is in Paris and is very capable, I think he will also be a great help to you.[7]

Trude Blau (later Amann) had already decided in the summer of 1936 to take part in curative education training at the Sonnenhof in Arlesheim. After March 1938 it was too dangerous for her to return to Vienna, and on Ita Wegman's advice she joined Karl König. During a short visit to Paris, Trude Blau and her friend Willi Amann, a lawyer and musician from Vienna, had their first chance to meet Peter Roth and Thomas Weihs.[8]

In the last days of August 1939, the chemist Alex Baum also received his visa for Great Britain. He had spent the months prior to this in a sanatorium in Paris faking tuberculosis with the help of a doctor friend in order to avoid deportation in case the Germans would invade.

Just like Thomas Weihs, Hans Schauder had the opportunity to complete his medical studies in Basel, Switzerland. While Thomas Weihs and his Swiss wife, Henny, were able to reach England on the last ferry before war broke out at the beginning of September 1939, Hans

Schauder, who had been ill with a protracted pleurisy, did not reach Scotland until 1940. He was helped and accompanied by his fiancée Lisl Schwalb, who had appropriate connections through her friendship with the Haughtons. Schauder later recalled this adventurous journey:

> A rail journey through France in 1940 was a phantom trip. The country was at war and completely blacked out. We travelled through France during the night and the whole of the country around us was shrouded in darkness. The train itself was blacked out. These surroundings accorded fully with my mood. I saw no light. Switzerland had adopted a reserved attitude towards me but despite all the terrible events happening around it, the country [itself] was a world of light and peace. Now we were travelling through a dark country under threat of war into an equally dark future. Lisl and I occasionally said something to one another – in German of course. Our fellow travellers completely froze us out because in some way they considered us to be the enemy. It was a surreal journey. The situation was the same as in the Vienna tram on the evening that Hitler marched into Austria when we were the only two without a swastika. Now, fleeing from the Germans, we had a similar experience. I experienced the feeling of being excluded as a supposed enemy on several occasions: by the Germans as a Jew, by the French and English as a German. In the end, my British passport finally brought me peace.[9]

Together with Karl and Tilla König, this group established the community in Scotland that would later

Kirkton House, the old vicarage on the Williamston Estate.

become known as Camphill. Apart from Tilla König, Ann Roth and Carlo Pietzner, all came from families with a Jewish background. However, most of them were familiar with Christianity and many of them had felt connected to The Christian Community in Vienna.

Kirkton House

Kirkton House, the empty old vicarage on the Williamston estate, was prepared for the new venture. The König family's furniture was on its way from Zurich, where it had been in temporary storage. Whilst Lisl Schwalb continued to live with the Haughtons, the first members of the group moved into Kirkton House on March 30, 1939: Tilla König, with her four children, and Alix and Ann Roth.

The following day, Karl König and Peter Roth also

Some of the members of the founding group at Kirkton House in May, 1939: Rudi Samojé, Marie Blitz, Ann and Peter Roth, Tilla and Karl König. In front: Peter Bergel, and Andreas, Veronika and Christoph König. Peter Bergel was the first child to be cared for at Kirkton House.

joined them from London. On his first night, König had a significant dream in which he saw a ship land on nearby Mount Bennachie:

> I saw a great ship, which I immediately knew to be Noah's Ark, landing on the summit of Bennachie. It anchored between the two peaks. Then the doors in the powerful ship's body sprang open, and a great crowd of people – men, women, children, large and small, old and young – streamed from the belly of the ark. They moved downwards from the summit and began to populate the land. I woke bemused and astonished. Was this a sign for our coming work?[10]

Every Monday, König went to medical school in Dundee to fulfil the requirement of his entry permit. This gave him the opportunity to improve his English and to broaden his medical knowledge, both in the university library and in the lectures. He also found time to deepen his professional insights from an anthroposophical perspective. König spent most of his Friday afternoons in Aberdeen, where Peter and Alix Roth's parents ran a guesthouse with a small convalescent home at Heathcot House on the River Dee. He spent hours holding his surgery there and then spent the weekend back at Kirkton House. On some weekends he also travelled to England to maintain contacts, but also to obtain residence permits in Britain for friends still in danger.[11]

König suffered a great loss in the autumn of 1939 when his friend Eugen Kolisko died suddenly of a heart attack. König, however, continued to feel an inner closeness to his departed friend: 'He has long been beside me as helper, admonisher and brother.'[12]

Ann Roth (later writing as Anke Weihs) described how the group missed König during his absences, but at the same time feared his criticism when he returned at the end of the week if their work did not meet his expectations.[13]

With her calming influence, Tilla König made sure that Kirkton House became more homely, and gradually a feeling of community began to grow. After about six weeks Peter Bergel arrived as the first child to be cared for at Kirkton House. His Jewish parents had obtained a visa for the United States but were not allowed to take their son with them because he had a learning disability. Peter Bergel was followed shortly afterwards by twenty-nine-year-old Rudi Samojé, a refugee who suffered from severe epileptic seizures.[14]

A few weeks later, the first two English-speaking boys arrived. The curative education work began with these four individuals. They were given lessons and therapeutic exercises, but the focus was mainly on integrating them into social life. Eventually, there were a total of twelve children

The children of the founding group in Kirkton House. Among them: Robin Linney (back row, second from left); Christoph and Renate König and Peter Bergel (centre), and Andreas and Veronika König (front row). The names of the other children are unknown.

and youngsters living in the house (including König's four children), for whom lessons, therapies and, soon, the non-denominational Sunday services were offered. The Quakers arranged for some of these children to be transported from Central Europe through the *Kindertransporte* which they organised.[15]

Marie Blitz and Trude Blau had already arrived in Scotland and were present at the official opening of Kirkton House at Whitsun in May 1939, which was also attended by some guests. Ita Wegman had sent her friend Kalmia Bittleston;[16] the Haughtons were also present.[17]

Karl König gave a speech that placed the initiative in the context of the Iro-Scottish cultural-historic stream, which was more than a thousand years old. This stream, flowing down from the northwest towards Central Europe had met with traditional Christianity coming up from the Mediterranean region. Now, Christianity stimulated by anthroposophy in Central Europe would make a cultural contribution in Scotland:

> We must understand this rightly. It is not that we should see ourselves as the bearers of a mission, but that we would try to bring about a meeting between everything that has been dreamt and thought by the German spirit and that which the English spirit can accomplish by way of deeds.[18] We should promise one another not to create an island of Central Europe here but to try as well as we can to act for the good of this land. We want to try to achieve this even in the knowledge that even if we fail, others will succeed. But let us try, and perhaps the spirit will allow us to make such contribution.[19]

Anke Weihs (formerly Ann Roth) described how in the early years König was the first person people turned to with their questions, but he soon encouraged his younger coworkers to work independently and provided comprehensive training and development for them:

> None of the young people … had much notion of Rudolf Steiner's teaching, for some it was alien. Yet [König] himself based all his work and striving on [Steiner's] teaching and knew that his future work for handicapped children would at all times have to flow from that source and no other. Therefore his young helpers would have to become pupils of Rudolf Steiner. But there was no force or coercion … Dr König steadfastly studied basic books and

> lectures with us, leading us step by step into a new world. In this world, he himself moved freely, was always creative, forward-going, courageous, and at the same time, he had an infallible way of preserving the integrity of Rudolf Steiner's spiritual science … But the accumulation of spiritual information and facts was not enough for Dr König, although he himself knew every single lecture that Rudolf Steiner had given, and there are thousands … He taught us never to live by theory, but to regard every minute of the day as an exercise to devotion, humility, creativity and the willingness to change oneself.[20]

Relocation plans

By the beginning of 1940, the entire founding group had arrived in Scotland. The last of them was Hans Schauder, who at first lived in the Haughton family manor with his new wife, Lisl, while he recovered from a severe bout of pleurisy. Everyone found it difficult to adjust to the demands of a curative life, especially as far as the physical work in the house and garden was concerned. In Vienna, this had often been done by domestic servants.

It soon became clear that the premises at Kirkton House were inadequate, and with the outbreak of war on September 1, 1939, misunderstandings between the new residents and the Haughtons began to arise over the new residents' responsibilities. Because no one at Kirkton House owned a radio, no one knew about the immediate blackout order, which was brought to their attention by the police the next morning. Anke Weihs later described how this image of the only house lit up in the dark of night remained inscribed in their hearts.[21]

Ita Wegman regretted the increasing estrangement

between the Haughtons and König. On January 18, 1940, she wrote to König: 'I really hope there will be no breakup with Williamston, that would be a real pity because we rely on each other for our progress.'[22]

However, having later heard from the Haughtons, Ita Wegman was more critical of König's lack of consideration and gratitude for his host's hospitality. In a letter to Frances Melland at the end of February, she wrote:

> There is no understanding between Dr König's group and herself [Mrs Haughton] and her husband, I think they are too strange for one another. Mrs Haughton is always willing to help, but she likes also to manage, and Dr König has the same tendency. But König is the stranger and should understand the circumstances and he must be grateful for the help he received. That matters are not going as they should makes me very sad for it will all be reflected back on Anthroposophy. Dr König has altered the house, which the Haughtons let him have free, without first consulting them, but told them after it was done … and my advice is that people do not just 'worship' Dr König, but that he understand that he cannot take liberties in a strange land where he is receiving hospitality.[23]

König, however, saw the situation differently:

> [A] certain tension developed between us and Mr and Mrs Houghton, due to national and cultural differences. The two Scots felt obliged to oversee our work and life, as they had active feelings of superiority toward all foreigners. They often treated us in the way the English were wont to treat natives in the colonies. Grave

> misunderstandings resulted from this behaviour, and some difficulties arose.[24]

With the outbreak of war, everyone in the founding group became 'enemy aliens'. They were, after all, still citizens of Austria, a country that now belonged to Nazi Germany.

In January 1940, the group heard for the first time about the Camphill estate in a suburb of Aberdeen. It consisted of Camphill House, the handsome main building, a small gatekeeper's lodge, and Camphill Cottage, which housed an old chapel and had a large garden attached to it. During one of König's regular visits to London, where he held consultation hours and examined children who applied for the small community, he met the publisher William Macmillan, who was the father of a child in need of special care. Macmillan was willing to buy the Camphill estate for the community and initially lease it to them, allowing them to buy it.[25] The move from Kirkton House was planned for the beginning of June.

Internment on the Isle of Man

On May 12, 1940, Whit Sunday, during the early days of the Battle of Dunkirk, the detention of male 'enemy aliens' in the UK took place:

> In Kirkton House, everything remained peaceful … The Whitsun message resounded from the altar and filled us with great joy. Then we took a Whitsun walk with the children and adults. When we returned, we were told that Frau Roth had called from Heathcot to say that her husband had just been collected by the police. All men with German and

> Austrian passports would be collected today and detained. We took in this news with astonishment and mild doubt at first. But as we sat at the festively decorated dinner table, the police came and ordered us men to dress and pack our suitcases in order to be ready for the transport in a half hour. Stunned silence fell on the coworkers and children.[26]

Married men were sent to the Isle of Man, unmarried ones to other camps; some, like Carlo Pietzner, Alex Baum and Willi Amann, were even sent to Canada. Some women who had passports from enemy countries were also interned on the Isle of Man in a separate camp. Even Rudi Samojé, the young man with a disability, was arrested because he had a German passport.[27]

The internees were placed in guest houses on the Isle of Man.[28] Escape was impossible because of the cold and stormy Irish Sea with its dangerous currents. Hans Schauder, who had only arrived from Switzerland in the spring and had lived with his wife in the country house with the Haughtons, described the atmosphere in the prison camp. It was characterised by the greatest contrasts:

> The British were unable to differentiate – and neither did they try – between Nazis, spies and Jews. Of course they placed those of us who were Jews into immediate danger when they locked us in the camp along with the Nazi Germans. It was very poorly guarded because the authorities thought that we would be unable to escape from the Isle of Man. The Nazis in the camp constantly spread rumours that German submarines would soon appear off the island and land weapons and soldiers in order to establish a base near Ireland in the forthcoming invasion of the British Isles.

Those of us who were Jews really were afraid on the Isle of Man. We continued to wrack our brains why the British treated Jews like Nazis. We could find no other explanation than that they considered everyone who had come to the island just before the outbreak of war and in the first days of the war to be Nazi spies. They made no attempt to categorise refugees who had some connection with German-speaking countries as anything other than spies. When we arrived at the camp, there were no interviews nor questioning of any kind to discover our background: we came from Germany and that was that … We were a colourful mixture of people, but we all got on well with each other. There were very well-known musicologists among us, including Otto Erich Deutsch, the great Schubert expert who set up the Deutsch index which is used in all references to the composers work … We were, on the other hand, interspersed with real idiots and convinced Nazis. One of them kept rushing out every time he heard an aircraft, shouting: 'They're coming, they're coming.' The Hitler supporters in the camp firmly believed that the Germans were coming with aircraft or submarines to liberate us, which of course terrified me and my friends. I can still recall a fine and elegant younger man called von Preussen. He was not related to the former imperial family but was an ardent nationalist for all his distinguished appearance who was ill disposed towards us Jews. It was a very curious situation for us: the Nazi Germans in the camp did not like us, were banking on Hitler's victory and saw the English as their enemies. The English accused us of being Hitler's fifth column, and we quaked at the prospect of a German victory and longed for the

> protection and help of the English ... The group of emigrants was the largest in the camp and that was perhaps the reason that the Nazis left us in peace. Open and aggressive antisemitism is dependent on a certain encouragement from the environment in which it occurs. In an English environment there simply was no open antisemitism. We did not discuss politics with the others, but we played music with them.
>
> One of our group was an exceptionally gifted musician, who later became a member of the Amadeus Quartet. I cannot remember how we acquired the instruments, but I can recall a performance of Bach's double concerto. One violin was played by this highly gifted young Jewish violinist and the other was played by the antisemitic von Preussen. It was a poignant moment for all of us. In Germany, a terrible barbarism had reared its head. Those of us who were Jewish had fled the destruction and were sitting here with the supporters and admirers of Hitler and heard our wonderful Bach with them and were suddenly united for a while by the music. I could not restrain my tears.[29]

About Karl König Schauder wrote: 'Dr. König was constantly nursing phantasies of breaking out of the camp'.[30]

On the island, König met people he knew through his anthroposophical connections before he emigrated to the UK, and who also lived in British exile. There was the possibility of meeting during the day for joint study and research. Particularly important for König was the friendly collaboration with the physicist and chemist Ernst Lehrs, one of the founding teachers of the first Waldorf school, and the astrologer Willi Sucher.

König also found time for artistic activities. He worked on his illustrations for Rudolf Steiner's *The Calendar of the Soul,* and wrote drafts for short plays that have been preserved as fragments.[31]

The move to Camphill

After the arrest of the men, the women were worried. How long would the war last? Where would money come from? When would the men be released?

Tilla König, Alix Roth, Marie Blitz, Trude Blau, Lisl Schauder and Ann Roth decided, after weighing the various options, to move to Camphill with the children on June 1, 1940. An exchange of letters with the interned men was possible, but all post was subject to scrutiny and censorship from the authorities and thus took a long time to arrive. Because of this, the women at Kirkton House did not receive König's letter advising them against the move until after they had made the decision.

In the summer and autumn of 1940 the Battle of Britain took place in which the Royal Airforce fought the German Luftwaffe, defending the UK against Nazi invasion. The north-east of Scotland was particularly affected by this. Anke Weihs described in her memoirs that many German bombing raids were flown in the area around Aberdeen. Camphill was close to the village of Peterculter, known locally as Culter, and only 8 miles (13 kilometres) from the coast. A church and a school were destroyed, and there were hundreds of casualties:

> German planes discharged their bombs in the fields around Culter on their way out to the sea … we were 'enemy aliens', and a regulation had been issued that no enemy aliens were to be allowed to

> remain within 10 miles of the surrounding coastline. (Camphill is 8 miles from the coast.) Whenever we answered the doorbell to an army or police officer, we expected to be told we would have to move.[32]

While the women were busy with the move to Camphill, the interned men prepared themselves for life in the future community. They wrote to the women regularly and supported each other as much as possible. Packages with sweets, clothes, books and painting utensils arrived from Camphill. Soon after moving in, the women received a letter from Karl König containing a small booklet with various contributions, poems and verses from the Gospel, which he dedicated 'for the courageous women of Camphill in love and gratefulness' in recognition of their brave decision to move.[33]

In connection with the Iro-Scottish monastic stream that had gone from north to south across Europe, König felt that a new imprint was now to be received in Scotland through the group of friends who had brought Central European culture in the opposite direction. He wrote a motto for the women, which the whole community later adopted:

> The truly wise one, o ye monks, works in such a way that each of his deeds is penetrated by the right inner attitude.
>
> If he is in the garden, then he is like a gardener.
>
> And when he speaks to the many, then his attitude is that of a teacher.
>
> When he works in the Community, then he works in such a way, that no orders will issue from his mouth, but his own doing will be ordered, so that it spreads order around itself.
>
> He will be a servant, rather than a leader, a silent

> one, rather than a loud one. A receiving one, rather than one who is sharing out.
>
> Thus, through his non-ordering he will create order. Through his receiving, he will be a healer. Through his silence, he makes audible the World-Spirit.
>
> Just this is needful.[34]

After friends in London lobbied for König's release, he was one of the first to be allowed to leave the camp on October 4, 1940. Peter Roth, Thomas Weihs and Hans Schauder were released from the internment camp on the Isle of Man several weeks later. The unmarried men Carlo Pietzner, Alex Baum and Willi Amann returned from Canada months later. Willi Sucher, Ernst Lehrs and his wife Maria Röschl-Lehrs, whom König had already met in Dornach in 1925 and who had been held in the women's camp on the island, came to Camphill after their release from the Isle of Man.

6
Camphill: Building a Community (1941–44)

Genius loci

Rudolf Steiner had advised the first curative teachers at the Lauenstein home in Jena to connect with the 'genius loci', the spirit of the place, and draw upon the spiritual impulses that had arisen there earlier. On the opposite bank of the Saale river from Lauenstein was a promenade where Goethe and Schiller had cultivated their friendship on many walks, encouraging each other in their work. Goethe had received inspiration for his fairy tale *The Green Snake and the Beautiful Lily* from there, and as a result the fairy tale came to represent not only the initiative at Lauenstein, but also the entire impulse of anthroposophical curative education that developed from it.[1]

But what story played a similar role for Camphill?

In the barren, hilly landscape by the sea with a view of the Highlands, settlements had formed early on along the River Dee. Iro-Scottish monks had settled in some places, and the standing stones, dolmens and stone circles on the hills and fields dated back to even earlier times. The connection between the locals and the natural world was also evident in the many 'fairy hills', the small, conical mounds in the fields and meadows that in Celtic folklore were believed to be gateways to the fairy world.

Karl König and his friends also discovered something else that was special about the surrounding area: the Camphill estate and the neighbouring village of Culter had been home to a settlement of the Knights Templar – a last refuge for a short time after the order had been broken up.[2]

König himself described the environment of Camphill and the relationship of its history to their own situation as follows:

> According to legend, the great Columba wandered through the Dee Valley, preaching and evangelising, and only from that time onwards did the land become fertile and abundant with flora … the remains of ancient stone circles and dolmens are embedded in the hills and knolls all around the Dee and Don. Everywhere one goes there is evidence of a prehistoric past … The River Dee flows into the North Sea at the outskirts of the city. It is accompanied on its long journey by the Dee Valley, a narrow, fertile strip of land extending to the north and south. Small suburban settlements can be found along the banks of the river; further inland they are more village-like … Camphill is situated on the north shore of the Dee, about 10 km [6 miles] upstream, in the hamlet of Milltimber. Originally there were three houses – the large manor house, the so-called lodge (the porter's house where the gardener lived) and a small farmhouse with adjoining barns and stables. A horse and cart were kept for the ladies and gentlemen of the manor; there were also a few cows. Grass and oats were

> grown in the estate's fields and meadows, and the garden – enclosed within high walls – supplied vegetables for the small group of people who lived there ... The great park of the Camphill estate stretched as far as the banks of the River Dee – the melody of the river's murmuring flow always to be heard in the south-facing rooms ... The fields and meadows of a similar estate – called Maryculter – spread out on the opposite bank of the river in a slightly western direction. Both Camphill and Maryculter were once at the centre of a powerful estate encompassing many hundreds of hectares. On the perimeter of Maryculter, sheltered within the fences of an ancient cemetery, are the graves of the Templar Knights who once occupied this land. They had been the lords and gentlemen of the immense and powerful estate and they lived at Camphill and Maryculter ... Camphill had been one of the northernmost settlements of the Knights Templar Order. The last remaining ambassadors of the Order were also murdered here, as everywhere else in Europe. Filled with malicious intent and greed for gold treasure, Philippe the Fair, King of France, had vowed to destroy the Templars. When (Jacques de) Molay, the remaining Grand Master was burnt at the stake on the Ile de la Cité on the Seine in Paris, the great Order was finally wiped out. The 'auto-da-fé' (judgement of faith) was carried out on March 11, 1314.[3] Hitler, an imperator of horror, marched into Vienna and Austria on March 11, 1938. This was also when the history of the Camphill movement began.[4]

The aims, ideals and history of the Knights Templar, whose full name was the Poor Knighthood of Christ and

Camphill House in 1953.

the Temple of Solomon in Jerusalem, became a recurring theme for the members of the community.

The beginning of a community

Karl König was the first of the interned men to return from the Isle of Man at the beginning of October 1940. Anke Weihs (still Ann Roth at the time) described how the women had gained a certain independence in their decision-making and the way they organised their lives during the men's absence. She described the situation created by the return of König and eventually the other men as follows:

> In the few months we had lived together in Camphill we had begun to establish ways of living and coping with our daily situation. Whereas the men had been able to devote themselves in a unique way to spiritual life in the camp, the women had stoked boilers, washed laundry, tended children,

> and worked the garden. We had been living in two different worlds. And so Dr König's coming constituted a stormy wedding feast between the male and female components of our community. But it was a valuable experience. Looking back it would appear that basic to the wellbeing of any community is the recognition of, and balance between, the archetypal male and female elements ... With the return of [the men] ... we actually began to use the word community in reference to ourselves.[5]

König's own view of the situation at the time is made clear in a letter to Thomas Weihs, who was still in the camp, dated October 24, 1940. The reason for writing was his joy at Thomas Weihs' decision to join the new Camphill community, as Hans Schauder and Peter Roth had done previously. This was a particularly difficult decision for Thomas Weihs, as his wife at the time lived with their young daughter in a house outside the community. König wrote of his various activities as a garden labourer, farmhand and house servant, the negotiations and efforts to secure the release of his friends, and the fact that he had been released from the obligation to attend university and could take the exams at a time of his own choosing. He reported on two planned events with the Reverend George MacLeod in Edinburgh and Glasgow whom he had met soon after his arrival in Scotland.[6] Following in the footsteps of Saint Columba (also known as Columcille), who had worked from the Scottish Hebridean island of Iona in the sixth century, McLeod had founded a new Christian community on the island in 1938.

Reading König's descriptions of the women at Camphill, you get an idea of what Anke Weihs meant by the 'stormy marriage between the male and female elements': community building was not only a long-term challenge to the understanding of gender roles at the time, but also required a mutual appreciation of complementary qualities:

> The women are all working very hard and with good will but the long months on their own were somehow almost too much for them and they need support, love and care. And I am not strong enough to cope with everything. But I am trying again every day ... It is strange for me to be now living solely among women and to experience this grandiose contrast to the previous male existence! I need to make a completely new start in understanding and grasping this different world; but it is a good learning experience. Everything goes on in love and kindness and only very rarely does the lion still have to roar. And he is very sorry afterwards.[7]

Karl König experienced a quality of love and kindness among the women that helped him to better control his dominant choleric temperament. He found this to be 'a good school'. He obviously regretted occasional outbursts of anger and tried to see them as an impetus for his own learning process. This not only led him to a certain self-knowledge, but to a realisation of the kind of social relationships and social dynamic necessary for community building.

Community life

Writing on the development of the movement, König described the early days of community life in Camphill:

> The household goods that had been brought along, the books and other possessions belonged to all of us together. It would have been intolerable and incomprehensible if one person were to have had a lot, and another little. And since we had no money, all of the work in the house, garden and fields was also seen as a shared task that had to be done. When the first children arrived and we thereby had increasing income, it was again self-evident: no one drew a salary, but we instead lived together in a kind of simple family association. Not only possessions but also money remained shared by everyone, and was used in a way that corresponded to everyone´s circumstances and needs. At the same time, we noticed that it was suitable to the children who had been entrusted to us to be surrounded by a life of this kind. To the degree that their forces allowed, they helped out in the house and garden, acquired practical life experience that had hitherto remained inaccessible to them, and began in this way to encounter the realities of daily existence.[8]

The idea of separating labour and income was in line with Rudolf Steiner's ideas on the threefold social order. However, according to Anke Weihs, it seemed premature for König to realise further aspects of this threefold structure in the community at this time:

> We first had to find and experience a threefoldness in ourselves and in our children before we could speak of a social organism. Nonetheless, it was during this autumn that we discussed the question of the compatibility of taking salaries with our spiritual-social intentions and came to the conclusion that to work for salaries would obscure

> our perception of the image of the human being in each other.[9]

Anke Weihs went on to describe how, in those early days in the autumn of 1940, they met every evening, often after work at 10 pm, until late into the night to discuss all aspects of community life: from the ordering of brooms and dustpans to the layout of the rooms and questions surrounding spiritual life. In the process, they got to know each other much better. On one of these evenings, König recounted a dream he had had on the Isle of Man on August 29, 1940, in which he had had a conversation with Count Zinzendorf. Nikolaus Count von Zinzendorf was the eighteenth-century Lutheran-Pietist theologian and founder of the Moravian Brethren. König had become familiar with the Moravian Church through his wife, Tilla, whose home village of Gnadenfrei in Silesia had been settled by the brethren. König had appreciated the simple life regulated by work and devotion. The settlements all shared similar working and living arrangements as well as a common occupation with certain Bible and song texts. As a result of this dream, König suggested introducing a weekly Bible evening. This was received hesitantly at first and only became an established practice in August 1941.[10]

In the final weeks of 1940, the seriousness of the war in Europe became increasingly clear, coupled with concerns about the persecution of family members and friends. This affected the mood of individuals, including König, as Anke Weihs recalled:

> Advent that year was dark inside and outside. Much of free Europe had been overrun by Germany. Inside, tiredness, frailty and some human difficulties had rendered us dull in consciousness and often it seemed we were trying to run a race with our feet

> glued to the ground. Dr König often withdrew from us in great gloom. But we performed the Nativity Play in front of ninety (!) people in Camphill House on December 22.[11]

It was also around this time that König developed closer contacts with the local education authority, and with the mayor and council of the city of Aberdeen. He was even given the opportunity to speak to the assembled city council in the town hall about curative education.

As a result of this, a long-standing friendship developed with James Downie Campbell. Campbell was a respected Aberdeen solicitor who had arranged legal matters when Camphill was acquired. He was then authorised to receive certain funds for Camphill as the official contact person of the Church of Scotland's Refugee Committee.[12] The local authorities sent the first children from the neighbourhood and so English became the language of everyday life. Among themselves, however, the co-workers spoke largely in German; moreover, Steiner's work, which they used for common study, was only available to a very limited extent in English. It was only after the war, when they finally adopted their place of exile as their home, that English began to dominate in all areas of work and social life.

At Whitsun 1941, a large conference was held on child education, attended by around one hundred doctors, teachers, social workers and parents. In the following months the community grew, and from Easter 1941 to the summer of 1942 the number of children increased to fifty.[13]

The first English-speaking co-workers found their way to Camphill, as did other Jewish refugees, including Therese 'Thesi' von Gierke (later Baum). Thesi arrived in autumn 1941 to help the König family with childcare as Tilla König was expecting another child. Unfortunately, the child was stillborn on March 11, 1942.[14] This date was already meaningful for both of them as exactly four years earlier the Nazis had taken Vienna, and in 1314 the last Grand Master of the Templars had been burnt at the stake. From now on, this date assumed a threefold meaning for König and his wife.

Annual festivals

Karl König wrote a play to be performed for Christmas 1941. It was based on the Christmas play he had sent his wife and children while he was in exile in London. He expanded it to include Adam and Eve and a few other characters who illustrate the evolution of humanity from the expulsion from Paradise to the birth of Christ. There was no distinction between actors and spectators; everyone took an active part in the celebration, singing together as they lit the candles on the Christmas tree.[15]

König wrote another play for the following Michaelmas, September 29, 1942, which he dedicated to the Camphill community. His plays were in the tradition of the medieval mystery plays, which had been cultivated in Central Europe, particularly in the *Wandervogel* youth movement. König gave his plays a pictorial, imaginative character and kept them simple with few scenes. Singing and speech choirs allowed everyone to be involved, the idea being that a practising community could form and experience itself through the rehearsals. The themes of the plays were rarely based on the classic content of the respective annual festival, but rather appeared, as in the Michaelmas play, as an enigmatic image. König himself often described their creation as a dreamy inspiration and how they seemed to come to him as if from outside, developing primarily in the realm of the night.

He sometimes experienced later performances as if they were completely new and was emotionally moved by them. In the Michaelmas play, he took up the fairy tale archetypes of the guardian, the mother, the prince, the knight, the maiden and the human being in the context of human development. His allocation of roles certainly also reflected his appreciation of the contributions made by certain members to building up the community. König assigned himself the role of the guardian and his wife, Tilla, the role of the mother. The role of the prince was taken on by Carlo Pietzner, that of the knight by Thomas Weihs and that of the everyman by Peter Roth. Ann Roth was given the role of the maiden.[16]

Regarding these plays, Hans Schauder would later write:

> König possessed great artistic talent which helped him to feel his way sympathetically into the being of the other person. Almost from the beginning, he accorded key importance to artistic work … He was a good actor and wrote small plays … also small celebrations for special occasions in which his favourite co-workers appeared as archetypal figures.[17]

Hans Schauder leaves Camphill

Around this time, however, differences began to emerge within the founding group concerning the relationship between the individual and the community. Some members around Hans Schauder and his wife, Lisl, broke away from the group in 1943. Schauder and his wife had spent his period of convalescence with Mr and Mrs Haughton at Williamston Manor, and both had only loosely been part of the group at Kirkton House. This distance was never completely overcome.

At the end of his life Schauder wrote:

> The requirements of the community took absolute precedence over individual wishes … The strong integration of one's private life into the community increasingly became a problem for Lisl and me. On the other hand, working together with poor refugees in a foreign country under the most difficult conditions, Dr. König succeeded in creating an institution in the spirit of Rudolf Steiner, who was little known at the time.[18]

When Heathcot House, which until then had been used as a guest house by the Roth parents, was rented for Camphill in 1942, Hans Schauder took over its management:

> Although I mainly taught music to the children there, I also [took] religion [lessons] and was responsible for their medical care … Despite my training, König did not see me as a physician. He saw us as helpers trained by him whose previous profession was of no relevance.[19]

Schauder was in fact a few years older than most of the others in König's group. Before emigrating, he had obtained his medical doctorate at the Psychiatric University Clinic in Basel with his dissertation *On the Question of the Therapeutic Possibilities of Music for the Mentally Ill,* which formed the basis for the later development of music therapy.[20]

In 1943, the group led by Hans Schauder decided to start their own facility in Garvald, near Edinburgh. Schauder wrote:

> Although I could clearly feel that I should leave Camphill, it was incredibly difficult for me to make

> the break. I suffered under König and yet could not divorce myself from him.[21]

In the decisive conversation between König and Schauder, Schauder acknowledged that König was certainly the best judge of what would be most favourable for the development of Camphill. But he also feared that:

> nothing would ever become of me if I was to continue constantly to bow to his will. He proposed that I should become his superintendent and continue to develop the musical side. He had a vision of the future in which Peter Roth would become a priest and lead Camphill spiritually while I took over the medical side, and Thomas Weihs looked after the external affairs of Camphill. Such a triumvirate represented a real temptation for me. Lisl was very worried that I might succumb to it ... I would have not left Camphill without Lisl's resolution and strength ... I would not have survived in Camphill. It was easy for König to hurt me. It was, nevertheless, necessary for me to pass through this phase as one of the stages of my life.[22]

Towards the end of his life, König himself wrote about Hans Schauder:

> In Vienna, he had been the focus of the old youth group ... A contemplative melancholy [temperament] made living with others difficult. He was one of the most talented of our youth circle.[23]

König described Schauder's wife, Lisl, as a shy person, who never completely succeeded in joining their cause.

König had certainly endeavoured to find a suitable task for Schauder as a doctor within the community, but he was unable to approach him and Lisl in a way that connected properly with them. Schauder was later a school doctor at the Rudolf Steiner School in Edinburgh for many years and laid the foundations for anthroposophically oriented biographical work with his pioneering approach on counselling.[24]

After Hans Schauder's departure, König and his wife, Tilla – a trained paediatric nurse – moved into Heathcot House so that they could be on hand to offer the high level of medical care required by the children living there.

Religious life in Camphill

Religious life played a major role at Camphill from the very beginning. On Sundays, three different short liturgical services were held for children, young people and adults, which had been created shortly after the founding of the first Waldorf School in Stuttgart in 1919 in connection with the free Christian religious education programme. In discussions and negotiations with the authorities, Karl König always emphasised that these religious Sunday celebrations, which had already been introduced in Kirkton House, were not to be understood as denominational. They were Christian in an overarching sense and were therefore suitable for all denominations.

The Bible evening on Saturday was used by the adults to prepare for the Sunday celebrations, with the Gospel reading for the coming Sunday being heard throughout the preceding week in the house community. In this organisation of Saturday evening and Sunday morning there was also a Christian echo of the Jewish Sabbath, which begins the previous evening. However, the simple meal that was held on these evenings, with bread and salt, juice or tea, and accompanied by communal conversation, first about world or community events and then about the Gospel passage for Sunday, was modelled on the love feast of the Moravian Brethren. The Gospel readings, in turn, were not chosen by lottery as was done in the Moravian Brethren, but for each Sunday of the year in advance and in line with the themes of the Christian calendar by König and those responsible for the Sunday services. There was also an opportunity to remember the deceased during the weekly Bible evenings – almost everyone at Camphill had experienced the loss of someone they knew.

Most of the members of the original youth group had also already become acquainted with The Christian Community in Vienna through the congregation founded there. The Christian Community had been founded in 1922 as a movement for religious renewal by a group of theologians, students and others with the help of Rudolf Steiner. The young people from the Vienna circle, most of whom came from Jewish families, were particularly attracted by the open atmosphere prevailing during the community's founding years and the work on the fundamental questions of Christianity. They felt just as welcomed with their Jewish background as other people did.

In Germany, The Christian Community was banned by the National Socialists in June 1941.[25] In Europe, active congregational life was only possible in Switzerland, the Netherlands and Great Britain. The founding priest, the scholar Alfred Heidenreich, and his wife, Martha Heimeran-Heidenreich, had already started to build up the new religious movement in Britain in 1929. He was also active in its international leadership. Heidenreich took advantage of the last opportunity to return to Britain from mainland Europe on September 3, 1939, but from then on he was separated from his wife and son.[26] In 1942,

Heidenreich visited König and Camphill for the first time. It was the beginning of a lasting friendship between the two men. On September 20, 1942, Heidenreich and König signed an agreement on mutual support for Camphill and The Christian Community in Great Britain.[27]

After his internment on the Isle of Man, Peter Roth, who had been prevented by the National Socialists from completing his medical studies, decided to train as a priest in The Christian Community. König had encouraged him in this decision and told him of his hope to found a pastoral-medical settlement. König's idea for this impulse came from his involvement in the founding of the Free School for Social Work in Eisenach. Alfred Heidenreich supported this idea, as the two young movements were very similar. In 1942, twenty-eight-year-old Peter Roth went to London to attend the English seminary of The Christian Community; he was ordained a priest by Alfred Heidenreich on October 1, 1944.

König also became friends with George Adams, another close associate of Ita Wegman, whom he had met during the World Conference on Spiritual Science in London in 1928.[28] During these years, the two men had co-operated more closely with each other. Adams also took part in discussions with König and priests from The Christian Community in 1943. This created a space in which the common endeavours of the Anthroposophical Society, The Christian Community and the Camphill community could develop in a free atmosphere.[29]

The death of Ita Wegman and the significance of Kaspar Hauser

On March 4, 1943, Karl König received some upsetting news. His mentor and staunch supporter, the woman who had helped orchestrate his escape from the Nazis, Ita Wegman, had died in Arlesheim. König was devastated. In the days that followed, he wrote down the thoughts that had lived in his soul during the preceding months as a requiem for Ita Wegman: a kind of literary memorial to his deceased mentor in which he not only honoured the life of this important personality, but also issued a warning in the light of the global situation. In twenty-five verses, he created a prose poem of intense imagery and emotion, into which he also wove the secrets of Kaspar Hauser's destiny.

Kaspar Hauser had caught the popular imagination when he was found wandering the streets of Nuremburg at Whitsun 1828. He was sixteen years old and it soon became apparent that he had been kept in solitary confinement his entire life, with food and water brought to him by a man whilst Kaspar Hauser lay drugged and asleep. As a result of his imprisonment, Kaspar Hauser's development had been held back. He was referred to as the 'Child of Europe', and it was rumoured that he was possibly of high aristocratic descent. Tragically, he was killed in Ansbach on December 14, 1833.

König had felt a great affinity with the figure of Kaspar Hauser and felt strongly that he was a kind of patron saint of children in need of special care. In this respect, he saw Kaspar Hauser as a guiding star for the Camphill movement.[30]

Shortly before Ita Wegman's death, a lecture cycle had taken place at Camphill on the occasion of the first 'lunar node' after Steiner's Curative Education Course.[31] König, who had learnt how to record horoscope constellations from the astrologer Willi Sucher who was staying at Camphill at the time, made some interesting connections between the horoscopes of certain days in Kaspar Hauser's biography and other fateful moments in history. In Section III of his Requiem, he explained that at the hour of Kaspar Hauser's death, as well as that of the poet Adalbert Stifter, the moon moved from the sign of Capricorn to that of Aquarius. In Section IV, he added that the same thing happened at Ita Wegman's death. In the Requiem, König established connections between different places and eras and other complex, sometimes enigmatic relationships.[32]

Growth and social life

König repeatedly found spiritual points of reference that helped promote social cohesion within the community and provided focus and motivation for people during this challenging time. The plays he wrote for the annual festivals played a significant role in this.

As well as the ones that have already been mentioned, König wrote another play for the St John's Day festival in 1943, called *A St John's Play,* which was performed in the open air in a large meadow. The play explores cosmic and human evolution through the figures of John the Baptist and the evangelist John. Audience members were also participants, holding hands in a large circle and singing. In the middle was a smaller circle of twelve players, dressed in the colours of the rainbow, each with a crown representing one of the twelve symbols of the zodiac.[33]

During the difficult war years and despite all the challenges, König remained in contact with other anthroposophical friends in the UK and managed to organise meetings with them. König also developed friendly relationships with several landowners in Scotland who were involved in biodynamic agriculture.

In the final years of the war the work was expanding, and a growing number of children had to be cared for:

A performance of A St. John's Play with Murtle House in the background in 1952.

Additional people, who were at first new to us, came to work with us and had to learn to embrace these social forms of living together and to fit into this. This was easier than we at first thought it would be. In this setting with children in need of special care, this seemed to be very feasible, as they motivated the reciprocal trust and good will of their caretakers. Additional houses were soon added to the first one, and the larger the circle of coworkers became and the greater the number of children and youth grew to be, the more it was necessary for the work to become more specialised. Curative exercises, therapeutic eurythmy, school instruction and artistic activities became configurated areas. Workshops were created, as well as gardening operations, a farm,

The big circle in A St John's Play at Murtle House with a view of the Dee Valley in 1952.

and much more. What had been something more general, in which everyone was willing to engage in all aspects of the work, now fanned out into separate areas ... How should the financial arrangements now be organised in order to take this development into account? From earlier experience, we knew that money had to be dealt with consciously ... Each house, whether large or small, became an economically independent entity ... Those who worked with each of these entities were co-responsible for income and expenses ... In this way the 'fundamental social law' can be implemented in an initial, if still imperfect, manner. This law was formulated by Rudolf Steiner ... in 1906, and states: In a community of human beings working together, the well-

> being of the community will be greater, the less the individual claims for himself the proceeds of the work he has himself done; that is, the more of these proceeds he makes over to his fellow workers, and the more his own requirements are satisfied not out of his own work done, but out of work done by the others.[34]

By 1944 it had become possible to acquire Murtle estate, just over a mile (around two kilometres) from Camphill. In the following months, the neighbouring Newton Dee estate also came on the market, which lent itself to new agricultural work area with so-called 'juvenile delinquents'. Both expansions were again made possible by generous loans from the Macmillan family. The work in Newton Dee began in Advent 1945, inspired by the idea of a pastoral-medical community with Peter Roth as priest and Thomas Weihs as doctor and farmer. These preliminary experiences were later incorporated into the first village foundation for adults in Botton Village, located in the North York Moors in England, in the mid-1950s.[35]

In these early days of Camphill, there was a sense of common destiny between the émigrés from Vienna and the children in need of special care. Looking back, König described this as follows:

> At the same time, we dimly felt that ... children with handicaps were in a position similar to ours. They were refugees from a society which did not want to accept them as part of their community. We were political refugees, these children social refugees ... The most important fact was, however, that these children demanded of us a special way of life. It was not only up to us to educate and train them;

> it was they, through the simple fact of their special existence, who asked of us qualities which we had to develop. They asked for patience, equanimity and compassion. They asked for an understanding of their particular ways and behaviour. Every day was for us a new trial in humanity and self-education. It was a tremendous opportunity which had been given into our hands.[36]

König explicitly included himself in these learning processes, although in some respects he was ahead of the others in terms of knowledge and experience. He was able to place these processes in a larger context and thus offer others helpful suggestions for their educational, social and spiritual development.

The guiding lights of Camphill

From the very early days of Camphill, Karl König drew on three historical personalities and the communities they founded to serve as guiding lights for the new movement: John Amos Comenius, the seventeenth-century Czech philosopher and pedagogue; Nikolaus Count von Zinzendorf, the eighteenth-century founder of the Herrnhut community, and Robert Owen, the nineteenth-century Welsh entrepreneur who campaigned for better social and living conditions for workers and their families. König emphasised that these past community efforts were by no means perfect in their implementation; they had even failed on the surface. But, as internalised impulses, they could provide orientation for the Camphill ideals, a leaven for its growth as a social organism.[37]

John Amos Comenius was bishop of the Bohemian-Moravian Brothers during the Thirty Years' War and had to flee Bohemia because of his reformed faith. He found temporary refuge in Poland, Holland and Sweden, but remained a refugee for the rest of his life. He was not only a theologian, but also a polymath who was particularly committed to education. He wrote the first primer for children, which helped them learn to read but was also intended to explain the world to them. For the education of adults, he developed the idea of a *Schola Pansophica* or the Pansophic School: a school of universal knowledge, which was to be open to all classes of society and provide instruction in Latin, philosophy, logic, politics and theology. König particularly appreciated Comenius' ideal of pansophy, the promotion of universal learning in the never-ending advancement of humanity. Nature was to provide the seeds for knowledge, religion and morality, and such a pursuit of wisdom would show humankind the way to Christ and the divine.

Nikolaus Count von Zinzendorf was a Lutheran-Pietist theologian who offered a group of Bohemian-Moravian Brethren refuge on his estate of Herrnhut in Saxony after they had been expelled from their home country. Zinzendorf travelled to England several times and also to North America, where he founded further settlements under the name of the Moravian Brothers.[38] In 1727 the statutes of the Brotherly Agreement of Herrnhut were drawn up which expressed Count Zinzendorf's ideals of a Christian community in which all aspects of daily life were dedicated to achieving fellowship with Christ. He celebrated this spiritual foundation with a sacramental meal. This was followed by the establishment of the so-called 'hourly prayers', which were performed alternately by the sisters and brothers of the community. This was in keeping with the tradition of the 'perpetual prayer' of the Iro-Scottish monastic stream, which had radiated from the monastery of Bangor in Ireland to

Central Europe at the end of the first millennium. König was impressed by how Zinzendorf relied entirely on the powers of the heart for this human community, and how he gave all his energy to it as a preacher.[39]

Robert Owen was a Welsh entrepreneur and the director of a large spinning mill in New Lanark near Glasgow in Scotland. He campaigned for good social and living conditions for his workers and their families, and built spacious and hygienic homes, schools, kindergartens and a hospital. This social experiment attracted worldwide attention, although a similar attempt in Indiana in the United States failed. Owen originated various social reform ideas, including the first health fund for workers, co-operatives where property is owned by a group on a pro rata basis, and trade unions, which originally championed the interests of disadvantaged workers. Robert Owen also fought for human rights to apply to all people and children. What impressed König about Robert Owen was his strong-willed nature. He was neither a great thinker nor full of religious feeling, but he was imbued with a spirit of compassion for humankind, combined with an earnest desire to do good.[40]

König's central concern for community building at Camphill was to renew and further develop the different impulses of these three historical figures through anthroposophy. He understood Comenius' pansophy as a living, holistic understanding of human beings and the world. For the formation of a Christian community, König wanted to focus primarily on the individual's cognitive power and not, like Zinzendorf, on religious conviction, because he saw this as a possible seduction through a feeling of being chosen. Finally, he saw Rudolf Steiner's fundamental social law as a fertilisation of Robert Owen's social reform ideas. König compared these three previous impulses with the gifts of the three kings: 'Comenius brought the gold of his wisdom. Zinzendorf offered the frankincense of his love. Owen gave the myrrh of his good will.'[41]

The inspiration from these three guiding stars then led to the 'three pillars' that decisively characterised social life at Camphill for many years.

An echo of the ideal of Comenius' philosophy not only lived in the constant endeavour for individual and social learning, but also crystalised in the 'college meeting'. Originally, the aim of the meeting was for all co-workers involved to understand a particular child in all their multi-layered facets, potentials, needs and support requirements. Occasionally, however, the joint pursuit of knowledge in such a meeting also involved a holistic insight into other fundamental questions concerning the community.[42]

Count Zinzendorf's impulse of Christian-religious community-building came to life in the daily prayers before meals, the morning and evening circles with verses and readings from the Gospel, which prepared the communal Bible evening on Saturday. This offered the opportunity for a quiet phase of contemplation, a social exchange over a simple meal that looked back on the events of the previous week, and a Gospel reading followed by a discussion that prepared for the religious celebrations on Sunday morning.[43]

Robert Owen's attempt at a new economic and social order was to find expression in a new way of dealing with property and money in conjunction with Rudolf Steiner's fundamental social law. Labour and income were to be separated from each other. The hope and expectation was that the individual co-workers would feel responsible for the whole, and that this could lead to the ideal of a fraternal economy between independent economic units such as house communities and workshops.[44]

Over time, all three pillars have changed due to social, political and societal developments. There are no longer any standardised patterns of organisation in Camphill communities.[45]

7
Developments and Transformations (1945–63)

Community motifs

Although the founding of the Camphill community in Scotland was determined by historical circumstances, by persecution and emigration, the original motives and impulses already lay in Karl König's work with the group of young people he met in Vienna. König played a central role in this social process, but he was dependent on the co-operation and support of the other members of the community, who played active roles themselves. The goal of creating a wholesome environment for people in need of special care was always paramount.

Artistic activities in the classical or educational-therapeutic sense were encouraged, and great importance was attached to the aesthetic design of the living areas. A special feature of life at Camphill were the annual festivals and, in this context, the plays written by König, in which he linked personal and social experiences with world events. The entire community was often involved in the staging of these dramas. Not only the actual rehearsals, but also the preparation of the costumes, the stage design, questions of directing, staging and musical composition became a process of forming and shaping the growing community. In the later phase of expansion, when new Camphill communities were created modelled on the original Camphill initiative, the traditions of celebrating the festivals and especially these plays were important elements. They helped to accelerate social cohesion at each new location: participants felt themselves to be part of a community, whilst at the same time the unifying Camphill identity was further strengthened.

The Easter play

A few months before the end of the war in the middle of January 1945, König wrote an Easter play in four parts.[1] These were performed on the evening of Maundy Thursday, Good Friday afternoon, Saturday morning and at dawn on Easter Sunday. The four parts gradually unfold a process of transformation, from death through to resurrection and renewal. The play begins on the evening of Maundy Thursday with a prelude in the middle of a cloudscape symbolising the spiritual region in which language originated.

For the part performed on Good Friday, König chose the story of the deportation of persecuted people with disabilities in ancient Athens, thereby alluding to the crimes of the Nazis. Near the Acropolis in front of the Temple of Zeus various people with disabilities assemble. One by one they engage in dialogue and learn to recognise each other and their needs through mutual compassion. A universal humanity is revealed in the way they complement each other as human beings. Nevertheless, they are considered outcasts and are awaiting deportation to an island. They experience the primordial Good Friday with the earthquake, the eclipse and the reappearance of the sun. All experience an inner overcoming of their respective limitations in their own way.

One of four Roman legionnaires who arrive to take the group away expresses this in the following closing words:

> Strange, strange –
> At first I thought
> We were driving off all of them
> As poor sinners.
> And now it seems to me as if I were following
>   them
> Not like a master
> Driving on the herd,
> But like a poor wretch
> Serving them.
> Strange, strange.[2]

The third part takes place in the late morning of Holy Saturday at the foot of Golgotha, in front of Christ's rock tomb. The sun is shining and silence reigns. There is an encounter between various characters from the Gospels: Nicodemus and Joseph of Arimathea meet the Samaritan woman, who recalls and reflects on her encounter with Christ at the well. Two high priests, three scribes, a Roman centurion and two soldiers who are supposed to seal and guard the tomb also appear. One of them muses at the tomb:

> How strange! Yesterday when I
> Saw you dying
> On the cross, you human being who is now
> Lying in the grave,
> You called out –
> It was just before the end –
> These words:

'Into thy hands, O Father,
I commend my Spirit!'
Since then these words
Have gnawed away in my heart ...[3]

The soldier is reminded of his homeland in Gaul, of the druids there and their special places of consecration. This foreboding leads to the final part of the play, which takes place in Ireland on the top of a hill near the sea in the middle of a druid sanctuary. It is shortly after sunrise on Easter Sunday and two druid pupils are about to spend three days at a sacred mystery site undergoing initiation. During the thunder and hail of a violent storm, they experience an inner vision in which they witness the resurrection occurring at that moment in Jerusalem. Their experience is confirmed by three druidesses in the temple, who experienced the extinguishing of the eternal sacrificial flames and felt the stones shake in the darkness. An old druid adds:

Creation is renewed
In the human heart![4]

The defeat of the Nazis and the end of the war in Europe on May 8, 1945, was celebrated in the streets of Great Britain on what would become known as VE Day, or Victory in Europe (the war in the Pacific against Japan would not end until August 15). With the liberation of Europe from the Nazis, the threat of persecution fell away, even if the extent of the suffering, terror and death was only slowly realised.

The post-war period

During the first summer holiday after the war, the first public doctors' conference was held at Camphill on August 6–9, 1945. It was attended by around eighty participants. König gave an opening lecture in which he spoke about bees as solar beings, and in the closing lecture he discussed the healing effects of certain substances, particularly gold. During the conference, on August 6 and 9, the atomic bombs were dropped on Hiroshima and Nagasaki in Japan. König's remarks, which placed the sun in a healing spiritual connection with gold, could be understood as running counter to the words spoken by the American president Harry Truman on August 8: 'The force from which the sun draws its power has been loosed against those who brought war to the Far East.'[5] Thirteen years later, in August 1958, König wrote the play *Book of Kells,* which he placed in the context of various Pentecost plays, but which he also dedicated 'For Hiroshima Day'. In this play, König wove together some of the ideas he had already expressed at the time with historical references to Iro-Scottish monasticism, especially to St Columcille, also known as Columba the Elder, and to St Brendan the Navigator, an early Irish monastic saint, known for his legendary journey to find the 'Isle of the Blessed'.[6]

During the war, only a few co-workers had joined the founding group in Camphill. These were mainly people who had fled persecution in Germany and Austria, although they also included people from other parts of the UK. Soon after the war, the first young volunteers arrived from many parts of Europe who had heard about Camphill and wanted to participate in the life and work of the curative education community. Many of them stayed, thereby allowing Camphill to expand.

For Christmas 1947, König further developed the 1941 Christmas celebration at Camphill into a community Christmas play that expressed hope and direction for an ongoing future development. The path of the divine word through the history of humankind, from Adam and Eve and through the patriarchs and the prophets, leads to the central event of the birth of Christ. However, König introduced a completely new theme by including a figure that represents human conscience, suggesting the effect Christ's incarnation continues to have on the development of human consciousness right up to the present day. Here, the forward-looking, future-focus of König's plays is expressed, as demonstrated in this call to the patriarchs to sharpen their sensory perceptions and thus open themselves up to what is new:

> Abraham,
> Look up!
> The Heavens again reveal
> What from you was closed.
> Isaac,
> Hearken!
> Peace enters into human hearts
> And fills the world with stillness.
> Jacob,
> Be aware!
> Good will in human limbs
> Brings freedom to the earthly world.[7]

After the German currency reform in 1948, it became possible for young people from Germany to travel abroad. This led to the first major influx of younger German co-workers to Camphill in Scotland. A report by König dates from this year:

> We now have 180 children to care for and educate … from Scotland, England and from the colonies, from South Africa, Kenya, [Sri Lanka] … The teachers and nurses, doctors and helpers, over sixty in number … have been brought together by further threads in the web of destiny. They [came] from Scotland, England, Ireland, Austria and Germany, from Bohemia, Holland, from Switzerland and Sweden. We all try together to create … an environment that is appropriate for the children in our care. They learn to work in the gardens, to plough the fields, to sow, to weave and spin in the workshops, to chop wood and to carve. In the kitchens they learn to cook and in the houses they learn housework skills; they learn to sing and to make music, to speak, to walk, to think. But the coworkers know that the children will only be able to learn when the teachers are prepared to educate themselves – if we learn to live with one another as a true community … And yet the self-education of a community is only possible if its members share a common ideal … the 'human image' in its physical, soul and spiritual form, is the star to which we aspire. It is our conviction that only by kindling the true image of man in our hearts will … we bring towards the children that which we can give them, [namely] lasting support and healing.[8]

Public interest in Camphill

Public interest in Camphill was sparked by an article that appeared in the *Picture Post,* a photojournalistic magazine which at the height of its popularity sold nearly two million copies a week. Called 'Where Love is the Cure', the article was accompanied by photos of Camphill taken by the Viennese photographer Edith Tudor-Hart, who had trained at the Bauhaus and emigrated to England and who occasionally worked for the magazine.[9]

At the beginning of 1949, Edith Tudor-Hart had contacted Karl König about her twelve-year-old son, Tommy, who suffered from schizophrenia. Her father and uncle had owned a socialist bookshop in Vienna with the affiliated Anzensgruber publishing house, which offered a wide range of books from workers' poetry and literature to treatises on the women's movement, sexual emancipation and educational reform. König was certainly familiar with the bookshop and the publishing house from his socialist-influenced youth in Vienna.

Edith Tudor-Hart visited her son every six weeks, staying in a nearby bed and breakfast. She was able to take part in Camphill life and was impressed by the landscape, the air, and the attentive care her son received. According to her great-nephew, Peter Stephan Jungk, König was happy for her to take photographs of the community. All the buildings were open to her, and she also took pictures of the surrounding park grounds, which are among her most impressive works.

This article, written by Scottish journalist Fyfe Robertson, appeared on April 30, 1949, and sparked a great deal of interest in Camphill. In the article Robertson wrote:

> Individual treatment is the chief secret of Camphill's successes. The basic treatment for all is good, naturally grown, balanced food; intelligent medical care, a serene and regular life, and above all, the affection which these children need and which sometimes make them flower wonderfully.[10]

The article led to a flood of enquiries from all over the English-speaking world, and the waiting list for places grew longer and longer.

St John's School and the Camphill Seminar

A small Waldorf school with its own building was soon set up for the children of co-workers and those from the surrounding area. St John's School was ceremoniously opened on October 12, 1948, by Karl Schubert, a friend of König's. Karl Schubert also came from Vienna and, as a teacher of the remedial class at the Waldorf School in Stuttgart, had been a participant in Rudolf Steiner's basic course on curative education.

In 1951 the school was expanded so that all the children at Camphill could attend. By then, König had already developed an approach to integration and inclusion. The children of each age group were to participate together in the main lessons, in which the age-oriented content of the Waldorf curriculum would be addressed. The aim was to speak to the higher spiritual nature – or entelechy – of the children, regardless of the physical circumstances and abilities of any individual child.[11] Being addressed in this way, he reasoned, should in itself have a certain therapeutic effect on the children. This could then be supported by curative approaches to education in the further lessons of the school day, normally reserved for specialised teaching. Thus, the main lessons would take place according to chronological age, and the further lessons in groups differentiated according to performance age with opportunities for special support and times for therapies.

In the years that followed, König repeatedly campaigned for the right of all children to education, which was not enshrined in law until much later in the UK.

The Camphill Seminar was founded in October 1949 in response to the influx of young people who wanted to work there, and König became the director of this training programme for anthroposophical curative education. In the first year, there were fifteen female and ten male participants who had been born between 1924 and 1930. Three of them had grown up in England, the others in Germany. Their childhood and youth had been overshadowed by the Second World War, and that of the Germans by the influence of National Socialism. Several had a connection to König through their parents, including Hartmut von Jeetze, whose parents had made Pilgramshain Castle in Silesia available at the time; Dorothea Stransky, whose parents, Ilse and Michael Rascher, came from Vienna and had helped to establish the curative education work in Pilgramshain, and Friedwart Bock, the son of The Christian Community priest Emil Bock. Many from this first intake remained at Camphill and later took on positions of responsibility in the Camphill movement when it expanded worldwide.[12]

The young newcomers formed a youth group within the Camphill community, creating similar experiences to those of the founding group. König wrote an Advent play for them in 1950, which was based on the parable of the ten virgins from Matthew 25:1: 'Then the kingdom of heaven shall be compared to ten maidens who took their lamps and went to meet the bridegroom.' The play takes up the call to be alert and to face unexpected challenges with presence of mind. It also clarifies that no one acts only foolishly or wisely, but that both elements are united in every person, and that the conflict between the two is fought out within the individual. Inner alertness is required, so that an inner connection to the spiritual world can be achieved and maintained.[13]

First visits to Central Europe

In 1948 Karl König was invited to give lectures in Holland in the autumn, and in April 1950, he went on his first lecture tour to post-war Germany. This was followed by many such tours, with regular visits to Switzerland and Austria. Hans Müller-Wiedemann described the ambivalence with which König was initially received:

> Who was this man, who as an exile in the British Isles had built up a community in the middle of the war and who now began to speak publicly in Germany in its aftermath? For many, the answer to this question – often posed in the early years after the war – arose from rumours and suppositions. König was a kind of mythological figure, a strange, legendary personality endowed with great powers of persuasion and eloquence; and only gradually did people begin to form a true impression of the nature of Camphill and who Karl König really was. For there were many rumours: enthusiastic approval or suspicious rejection. But it was largely due to König's journeys to Germany after the war that a large number of young searching people, who had experienced the war and National Socialism as children and adolescents, joined the group around König in Scotland.[14]

Camphill's founding group had consisted primarily of refugees of Jewish origin from Vienna. Now young people from Germany, who had spent their childhood and youth under the Nazi regime, came to know them and the life they had made for themselves during their many years in exile. Hans Müller-Wiedemann described these encounters as remarkable, often dramatic, but nevertheless fruitful for everyone involved. A mutual learning process unfolded through the daily tasks of curative education, which had as their focus a holistic view of human beings and the picture of development as described by anthroposophy. He continued:

> It seemed that this encounter could only take place in the light of anthroposophy. This gave Camphill in those early post-war years – although veiled beneath the surface of daily life – the character of a continual yet unexpressed healing of the wounds of destiny. An extraordinary, spiritual space came into being … But what visibly permeated those years in Camphill down to life's every details was the culture of Central Europe, a culture saved from destruction and now also open to new impulses from those who came as seekers. It was in the sense of such a spiritual space of hope that König tried to work in the German-speaking world after the war. The Central Europe that had gone into exile spoke through him, and people took notice.[15]

New tasks and separate paths

In these first years after the Second World War, Karl König also intensified his lecturing activities and working contacts in the UK. At the same time, he was appointed medical adviser at St Christopher's School in Bristol. In May 1949, Wraxall House, a residential home for the school, was opened there and König was asked to help find someone to manage the home. It was at this time that the lease on Heathcot House in Aberdeen expired, and due to its desolate condition the house was to be demolished. Tilla and Karl König had to decide where they would live from then on. To accommodate the many new children, Cairnlee estate near Camphill was acquired in early 1950.

Tilla König felt drawn to the task at Wraxhall House. It became apparent that her husband would be travelling a lot due to the many requests for his advice on the expansion of the work, and would only be able to spend certain periods of time with her. This could just as easily be the case in England as in Scotland. So, in 1950, Tilla König moved first to Wraxhall House and then to Thornbury, where a residential home had been set up for the children of Camphill co-workers who attended a neighbouring Waldorf secondary school. This also enabled her to contribute to the care of children with cerebral palsy at the newly founded Camphill School Thornbury Park. There was also a plan for her to be involved in setting up a training programme for nurses, which only later became a reality.[16]

König moved to Camphill House, the main building on the Camphill Estate, in 1949. He lived in a suite of rooms at the end of a wing on the first floor. His writings, work materials and extensive specialised library were kept in an anteroom, whose fireplace also heated the living room and bedroom behind it. The actual living room contained a folding couch, which served as his bed at night, a table and chairs, a large bookcase and his desk. The two windows gave him a view of the walled kitchen garden and the nearby River Dee, as well as the rose garden, which was later turned into a small cemetery, and the large trees on the main driveway. Some younger children with more complex needs and who were particularly close to König's heart, were also accommodated on the same floor. Downstairs, two rooms were set up especially for the so-called Camphill Goethe Library, for which König provided a basic stock of books and which soon developed into a large bilingual library with a lending system. He liked to have his main meal at lunchtime with guests in the large kitchen of the house. König's surgery room was located on the ground floor, connected to his living quarters by a small staircase so that he did not always have to use the busy main stairs. Since his death, König's rooms have remained as an archive and retreat for studies.

On the occasion of their twenty-fifth wedding anniversary, Karl and Tilla König travelled to Vienna, where they visited familiar places. On May 2, 1954, he noted in his diary:

> the bitterness of seeing Vienna again is great ... and to see everything again that is really home. The memories of my youth arise and the first springtime, and also the light and the spiritual fullness of this landscape. Seeing the 'city' again ... is also good. In the evening I sit with Tilla in a wine cellar restaurant and we have a peaceful supper and drink a good glass of wine together. So it's a real reunion after all.[17]

Two days later, after a walk past their old home, König reflected:

> It has all become foreign to me ... it was just a stepping stone, and the second time Vienna (1936 to 1938) was no longer the first. I was no longer 'myself' but had become a tool that prepared the 'community'. For Tilla, however, it was different. For her, it was all about family, children, the immediacy of life. This is how the gradual distance came about.[18]

The actual silver anniversary of the wedding took place the following day on May 5. The evening before, the couple had met Emil Bock, who had married them in 1929.

König wrote in his diary for that day: 'Now this is our 25th wedding anniversary. There are many telegrams, flowers and presents. Tilla is very quiet and content and I am happy for her happiness.'[19] To celebrate, they bought tickets for the evening performance of Johann Strauss' operetta *The Gypsy Baron*. Before that, they visited Leopoldstadt, König's old home:

> It rains in the afternoon and we walk through the city, past St Stephen's Church, into the 2nd district. It is a place of horror; the worst destruction in the worst district. It's hard to understand how dilapidated the alleyways and streets are. I'm glad to be outside again. In the evening at the Volksoper. *The Gypsy Baron:* and that adds the rest to all the unreality that surrounds us here. The performance is good, but everything is still empty, of the past, film-like, like a memory, but the one who remembers is no longer there. Tilla feels the same and we drive quietly back to our hotel.[20]

Two days later, the two flew back to London, where Camphill was given use of rooms in a flat in Harley Street for overnight stays and where König held regular consultations when he was visiting. Regarding their last morning together in Vienna, König wrote that evening in London: 'For the last time, Tilla and I are now sitting at the cosy breakfast table ... Somewhere in the background Vienna and Austria must be alive, but I can't quite find them.'[21] The following day they went in different directions again: 'I had breakfast with Tilla and then took her to Paddington Station. She is sad now and I can't help her much.'[22]

Nevertheless, despite living apart, there always remained a deep inner bond between König and his wife. They visited each other regularly several times a year, and often spent Christmas together with family members joining them. Every year Tilla would give him notebooks that she had bound herself for him to write his diary entries. They phoned each other regularly and were in constant correspondence.

Their eldest daughter, Renate, later gave her assessment of her parents' relationship. She described a conversation she had had with her father in 1965, towards the end of his life, during a stay in Botton Village where Tilla König was living at the time. When Renate asked him why he couldn't live with Tilla, her father replied openly – probably in recognition of his own melancholic tendencies – that his wife's melancholy would be too much of a burden for him in the long term and that he could only cope with it for a few days at a time. Her mother, on the other hand, took this as her cross, which she bore with inner strength for herself alone. She remained faithful to her husband throughout her life; her daughter never heard her say an unkind word to him or about him.[23]

König's intensive lecturing activities, combined with the many trips to various European countries in the early 1950s, and later to both the USA and South Africa, meant he needed help coping with his enormous workload. Alix Roth took on the role of private secretary, handling his extensive correspondence and managing various organisational tasks. When König was diagnosed with heart disease at the beginning of 1955, nursing duties were also added. Alix Roth had been his patient as a young woman in Vienna. She was very withdrawn and hardly spoke, and König had helped her to find her place in the founding group. In the early days of Camphill, she wrote to a friend that she saw König and Tilla as her new-found parents. Alix Roth tried to return the trust that König had placed in her and her self-healing powers, which allowed her to play her part in the fulfilment of König's further life tasks. In a letter from Christmas 1952, König thanked Alix Roth for this mutual inner loyalty and for the fact that she had never expected anything from him that he could not have decided to do out of inner freedom and insight. She would trust his angel even more than he would himself.[24]

Research, therapies and arts

As a researcher, Karl König pursued his medical, scientific and zoological interests throughout his life – in particular, embryology, physiognomy, animal studies and curative educational phenomena and diagnostics. He built on the studies on homeopathy from his time at the Vienna Institute of Embryology and set up a laboratory for remedies at Camphill in 1950. In collaboration with the pharmacist Rudolf Hauschka, he developed a remedy made from gold, frankincense and myrrh, which was marketed under the name of Thalamos.[25] As early as 1942, when the first children with Down's syndrome came to Camphill, König made this clinical picture the focus of his research.[26]

Anke Weihs had also met König as a patient in Vienna and even then had experienced his serious gaze, which radiated enormous warmth, as healing. She observed how the children in need of special care were also affected:

> Dr König was not a bit sentimental and he expected the most, even of a disabled child. … The peculiar power to call people up to their better selves and thus to create the first condition for healing reminded one of Socrates' description of himself as a 'midwife', helping to bring to birth the higher self in the other.[27]

König always saw anthroposophy as an extension of his perspective, and a way of embedding his scientific research in a larger context of meaning. As Anke Weihs explained:

> Few men were so well informed as to the medical developments of his own time and he never hesitated to acclaim or make use of what he found valuable in modern scientific research.[28]

As a doctor and curative educator, König always felt directly committed to treating his patients. The Greek word *therapeia* means service, care, and encompasses all healing measures, which are always preceded by a medical diagnosis. The entire organisation of community life at Camphill was intended to have a healing effect with stable social relationships, daily, weekly and annual rhythms, religious celebrations, annual festivals and artistic experiences. In addition, specific forms of therapy were prescribed on an individual basis. The eurythmist Irmgard Lazarus came to Camphill in the early 1940s, and together with her, König developed specific forms of therapy for individual children.

Susanne Lissau, later Müller-Wiedemann, came to Camphill at the beginning of 1948, and many of the children benefited from the fruitful collaboration that developed between them in the fields of curative eurythmy and music therapy.

In 1951, König invited Ilse Rascher, a colleague from Pilgramshain, to Camphill. Together with Elisabeth Löwe, she developed special therapies for blind children, including colour-light therapy.

Over the years, other therapies were introduced at Camphill, including rhythmic massage, painting therapy, speech therapy, play therapy and riding therapy.

In his youth, one of König's many career aspirations

Heathcott Chapel, a converted steel shelter on the Camphill Estate, where light-therapy sessions were held.

Coloured light therapy involves eurythmy movements performed behind veils with different light effects. They are usually accompanied by lyre music. The changing colours are caused either by differently coloured panes of glass or transparent films in combination with daylight or electric lights.

had been to become a conductor. The arts played an important role throughout his life and continued to do so at Camphill. König enjoyed playing the piano, often as a duet with Peter Roth or Susanne Lissau. He supported the artistic activities of his colleagues and greatly appreciated the fact that the founding group included both Anke Weihs, a dancer, and Carlo Pietzner, a versatile artist. Other artists and craftspeople joined later, including the Hungarian architect Gabor Tallo. König also contributed his own ideas and inspirations to the realisation of a large hall, a chapel and also the design of furniture and other artistic projects around Camphill.

Karl König's work and the legacy of the Third Reich

From 1925 onwards, Karl König published regularly in medical journals and various anthroposophical journals. In the years after the Second World War, he wrote numerous books, the best known among them are *The Human Soul, The First Three Years of the Child* and *Brothers and Sisters.*[29]

König's work also includes references to some German-speaking scientists of his time whose relationship to National Socialist ideology must be viewed critically today. They include psychiatrist Ernst Kretschmer, paediatrician and curative educator Hans Asperger and paediatrician Werner Catel. In the immediate post-war years, many people who had been complicit in the crimes of the Nazis tried to cover up their involvement. They tried to obtain 'clearance declarations' that would allow them to continue in their professional careers. It was not until the late 1960s and early 1970s that a serious historical reckoning with National Socialism began in West Germany. Starting in the early 1980s, the social pedagogue Ernst Klee began to detail the Nazi euthanasia programme for the first time.[30] German reunification in 1990 also made the archives of the former East German republic accessible for academic research. This led to new historical insights and assessments, especially about the often-unbroken continuation of professional careers from the Nazi era. During König's lifetime, however, this knowledge about the involvement of doctors in Nazi crimes was largely unknown.

In 1921, Ernst Kretschmer had drawn up a typology for certain male constitutions that had established a connection between body shape and susceptibility to certain mental disorders. In 1929 this research had earned him a Nobel Prize nomination. During the Third Reich, however, Kretschmer had worked as a judge at the so called Hereditary Health Courts in Marburg and Kassel and was responsible for ordering forced sterilisations. Most likely he used his typology for selection purposes.[31] König, ignorant of Kretschmer's role in the Nazi era, referred to the psychiatrist's constitutional typology in the lectures he gave in 1962 on social-therapeutic community building, often known as the 'Village Lectures'. König did not want such typologies to be taken 'as absolutes' but instead attached importance to not losing sight of the individual behind the type.[32]

In May 1954, during a visit to Vienna, König had the opportunity to meet Hans Asperger[33] and visit the curative education ward at his paediatric clinic: 'I had a good conversation with Professor Asperger. He is very friendly and interested and we talked to each other for a long time.'[34]

That same day, there was also a joyful reunion with König's old friend Paul Regenstreif, whom he knew from his anthroposophical work in Vienna. Regenstreif had also been persecuted because of his Jewish origins and had gone into hiding in Hungary during the Nazi era. Regenstreif's second marriage was to doctor Hildegard Buller, who in turn worked closely with Asperger. Three days later, König noted:

> Then in the evening with Prof Asperger … there is a very long conversation about curative education. Although Asperger is open and makes a great effort to understand and although he is a Catholic believer, many things remain closed to him. How is it possible to overcome scientific materialism? It is packed into people's bones.[35]

Despite this somewhat sceptical assessment, König wrote in a letter later that day, 'I also spoke with Professor Asperger twice at great length and in a positive manner'.[36]

König had also received data from Asperger during his visit for his study on Down's syndrome. On the day after his return to Aberdeen, König noted:

> In the evening I begin to write down the data on the … children that I received from Professor Asperger and compile it correctly. I am very much captivated by this miserable search for statistics.[37]

From then on, Paul Regenstreif and his wife, Hildegard, acted as a bridge between König and Professor Asperger. Asperger welcomed the fact that Hildegard was planning a three-month stay at Camphill at the end of 1955, and he also recommended 'only an anthroposophical curative education centre' to be the most appropriate for a particular child.[38]

König had planned to travel to Austria in 1957 to talk about curative education, but in the end the trip did not materialise. Paul and Hildegard Regenstreif had visited Camphill in the meantime and now they started planning a trip to Austria for the summer of 1959, with the intention of visiting places connected to Rudolf Steiner's youth. Paul Regenstreif wrote to König saying that Professor Asperger would like to meet him in Innsbruck that summer. König sent an immediate reply saying that he would also like to meet the professor.[39]

On January 27, 1959, Regenstreif passed on Asperger's request for König to give a lecture at Innsbruck University Children's Hospital on May 7 on the subject of teaching experiments with severely sensory impaired children. König accepted and enclosed a carbon copy of his acceptance letter to Asperger in a letter to Regenstreif on February 3. He wrote:

> I am very glad that Asperger has taken this step and hope that this lecture will be of significance for the whole development of our curative education.[40]

It remains unclear what exactly happened between König and Asperger in Innsbruck or what might have been discussed. A letter from König to Regenstreif in June 1959, only states:

> There is a lot to say about the stay in Innsbruck, because the aftertaste is quite bitter. But I don't want to write about that because it would be a bit painful. But I do believe that Asperger will do everything he can to keep our work out of Austria, as he doesn't want his curative education throne to start shaking. But that's only one side of the matter, we'll discuss the other verbally.[41]

However, just a few weeks later, a visit by Hans Asperger to Scotland seems to have gone very well. Through Regenstreif we hear of Asperger's reaction: 'Professor A. came back, who, as Hildegard wrote to me, was extremely enthusiastic and positive about his impressions of you.'[42]

König replied:

> the impression we all had was very positive. Asperger was extremely human, friendly and kind. He gave a delightful talk ... You know that Asperger doesn't say very much about what he thinks, but I had the impression that the way he walked around here and saw the essentials, he could sense what it was all about. We are all very grateful for his visit.[43]

While König showed a differentiated approach to typologies in his reference to Ernst Kretschmer, and a pragmatism characterised by ambivalence in his dealings with Hans Asperger, his clear judgement came to the fore in his debate with Werner Catel.[44]

In December 1957, König received a letter from Catel, the head of the paediatric clinic at Kiel University, inviting him to give a lecture on curative education at German Therapy Week in Karlsruhe in September 1958.[45] König gladly accepted the invitation and sent some of his publications to Catel. A lively and friendly exchange of letters and publications ensued, in which the content of the lecture was discussed. Catel particularly praised König's approach of 'feeling secure in the family' at Camphill and looked forward to a personal conversation about this. He wanted to know whether König agreed that in the case of so-called *Gemütsleere* (literally, 'emptiness of mind') curative education could offer no help.[46] Catel further explained that he believed that the soul was basically genotypically or genetically determined.[47]

In his reply, König emphasised a more positive attitude, stating his belief that mental and soul qualities could be revitalised and encouraged to a very large extent.[48] Peter Selg explains that as early as the 1920s, König had clearly distanced himself from claims of 'emotional emptiness' or 'emptiness of mind' and also from the theory that the soul is 'genotypically' determined. In his lecture in Karlsruhe, König explained that he had never met a child who could not be treated in some way, he expressly opposed outdated terms such as 'idiocy' or 'congenital imbecility', and spoke in favour of regular school attendance for all children with few exceptions.[49]

The correspondence between Catel and König continued and in September 1959 they met in person for several days in Sils Maria in the Swiss Engadine mountains. Despite their contrasting views, there were still certain similarities in their professional and personal interests. Catel arranged all kinds of contacts with German medical and scientific institutions for König and invited him to the Kiel paediatric clinic, where he hoped to draw on his curative education and therapeutic expertise for the treatment of certain children. They must also have had in-depth conversations in Sils Maria, as Catel wrote to König in April 1960:

> You are a great artist of life, I very much hope for you that you can – as you said in Sils Maria at the time – devote at least two hours a day to the 'inner man of the heart', as the evangelist puts it. My thoughts are often with you.[50]

In the summer of 1960, König was travelling in the United States for several months when a criminal charge brought against Catel for his activities in the Reich Committee for the Scientific Registration of Serious

Hereditary and Congenital Suffering was reported in the German press. The Reich Committee was set up by the Nazis in 1939 to carry out child euthanasia. All infants and young children with severe congenital diseases were registered. By the end of the war, the committee had compiled reports on approximately 100,000 children, with around 5,000 of them falling victim to these infanticides.

On his return to Scotland at the beginning of October, König received a letter from Catel in which he said:

> I hope that you have not lost faith in me due to the news of a truly mendacious and sensationalist press … But the day will come when I will seek vindication on a higher spiritual plane.[51]

He announced that he had submitted a request for early retirement. König was initially sympathetic and could not imagine Catel being involved in the killing of children. Catel was relieved that König had not turned against him.

At the end of March 1961, however, criminal proceedings were finally initiated against Catel. In 1962, he published *Grenzsituationen des Lebens* [Borderline situations in life], in which he set out his views on euthanasia. Catel attempted to approach the subject from a philosophical-historical perspective, including arguments in favour and against, but reaffirming that he was in favour of euthanasia if all those responsible were in agreement.

Catel sent a copy to König, who read it whilst on a boat trip to the United States in the summer of 1962. König wrote in his diary shortly after he began reading the book: 'completely inadequate and misleading.'[52] This was followed the next day with: 'He sent it to me and in it he tries to justify himself to himself.'[53] After reading the book Karl König wrote a review for the anthroposophical cultural and scientific magazine *Die Drei.*

The following summer, in August 1963, König wrote in his diary:

> Continue writing the euthanasia essay and can finish it. It is full of attacks against Catel and his attitude, but it seems necessary to me to point out the moral of this work and to characterise it in its way of thinking.[54]

For the autumn issue of *Die Drei,* König wrote to the editor:

> You will receive ... for the September/October issue an essay on the question of euthanasia following an unfortunate book written by Professor Catel. I had the impression that we would have to comment on these problems in *Die Drei* at some point.[55]

König asked for a prominent placement of his review and 100 offprints.

In 'The Problem of Euthanasia: A Word on Catel's Impossible Book', König mentioned that Catel had personally sent him the book 'in admiration and solidarity', made reference, among other things, to photos reproduced by Catel and other reviewers, but also took a general stance on the social Darwinist atrocities of Nazi medicine:

> At the beginning of 1962, a dubious book appeared which endeavoured to advocate the 'humane' killing of life unworthy of life ... Each of these photographs is ... only apparently true; they are misleading because – as Hellbrügge rightly points out – a large proportion of the 'monstrosities' shown

> are not viable. Even without 'limited euthanasia', they would die in the first days or weeks after birth. The three other children who are presented to the reader in this reprehensible panopticon look at us from sad eyes and evoke no sympathy other than that of wanting to help. Catel, however, wants us to believe that these are 'irrational beings' who are nothing but a *massa carnis,* a lump of flesh ... Catel's moral integrity must not be taken into consideration here, I do not know whether he placed himself at the disposal of Hitler's henchmen; it is not up for discussion here either. His writing alone is to be discussed...
>
> Why was it possible for racial mania to take on such forms? ... [Because] a supposed science postulated and propagated the idea of the 'struggle for existence'. This false 'evolutionary idea' was inoculated into social life, combined with the mysticism of racial hygiene and brewed into the poison that gave hundreds of doctors and their actions the documents with which they believed they could justify their shameful deeds to themselves and to the world.[56]

König not only firmly rejected Catel's approach to euthanasia, but also called for a holistic view of humanity based on an understanding of the immortal, spiritual essence of all human beings. This would form the basis of a future medical ethics.

At the time the review was published, König was on a lecture tour in Central Europe. It was not until the beginning of December 1963 that he sent a reprint to Catel, with whom he had not been in contact for a year and a half since receiving the latter's book in 1962. In the enclosed letter, König explained that the result of his review had been negative and that Catel would hopefully understand that the criticism was aimed at him as a representative of a certain school of thought and was not referring to him personally. Catel reacted with indignation and demanded that all remaining copies of the magazine and offprints be handed over, but he was unable to legally enforce this.[57]

8
The Last Years (1963–66)

Karl König's life unfolded in close connection with the development of Camphill and was sometimes almost inseparable from it. He received great recognition for his work and was valued as an exceptional personality. At the same time, he could always be experienced as an ordinary, everyday person in the context of community life. His own writings and the reports of others make it clear how much he struggled with himself, his physical and mental weaknesses, and how he found the courage to move forwards only with the greatest effort.

Throughout his life, König had to come to terms with his unusually small stature, his congenital walking disability and the orthopaedic footwear he needed. He was dependent on support for many activities. In a diary entry from October 1965, a few months before his death, he reflected on his physical constitution during a train journey: 'There is a man in the compartment who is as small as I am and I have to think about what it means to be incarnated in such a form as we both are.'[1]

Anke Weihs gave an impressive description of his appearance:

> Dr König himself was a natural example of co-ordinated movement. For although he was

> unusually small, his feet having a slight impairment since birth, his bearing was remarkably free and there was a hidden grace in his gait. When Dr König lectured, he paced to and fro, the words seemed to come with his strides. When he spoke about animals, a dear subject, he would with one characteristic gesture become one or the other animal, to the infinite delight of his audience.[2]

Karl König possessed a choleric temperament coupled with enormous willpower and great stamina. But there were moments when he suffered from his choleric behaviour and sank into deep, depressive, melancholic moods; he was often plagued by self-doubt. The enormous extent of his workload, his plans and intentions weighed on him:

> In the evenings, together with Alix, I tidy up all the folders of my previous work, and the amount of what I have done, but especially that which I still have to do, looms over me. When will I have the concentration to complete these heaps of unorganised and aphoristic work, which seems ingenious, but is not really ingenious at all? Or should it not be completed at all [and] remain only piecemeal like myself?[3]

He also struggled with insomnia, headaches and migraines. The following extracts from his diary give examples of this:

> It is a dark day, filled with headaches and nausea … I cannot overcome my inner resentment and am overcome by doubt and darkness.[4]

> I experience myself as a stranger among people.[5]

> The night was bad again and in the morning my resentment is so great that I am full of anger and accusation. I can't do my exercises or pray and an otherwise unknown cynicism pervades me. I feel beaten up by the spirit and instead of being grateful, I rebel and shut myself off with stupid pride and false indignation.[6]

Christoph Andreas-Lindberg, a colleague of König's for many years, once described him in the following way:

> Dr König could be a difficult person to approach. Yet every time, on entering his room, one was at once reassured by his welcome. He seemed to know you, and in the brief time allotted, mostly half an hour, unspoken doubts were dispelled and superficial analyses of a situation corrected. Meeting him, one felt warmer … through being recognised.[7]

Anke Weihs recalled König's outstanding qualities, such as his love of order and diligence, which enabled him to cope with his enormous workload in a very disciplined manner:

> Dr König had an outstanding power to create and maintain order … He was extremely punctual and would not accept unpunctuality in others … Dr König was an example of careful preparation … He laid aside other issues, cleared his mind and was simply ready to receive. He never came to a meeting looking as though he were preoccupied with something else … he never did things hurriedly, however urgent.[8]

Anke Weihs also described the different sides of his choleric temperament:

> He was at times an 'enfant terrible', but he had as well a delightful and redeeming sense of humour ... He demanded great earnestness where earnestness was appropriate, but he could ridicule the 'long face' in no uncertain terms. Laughter is as essential to community living as anything else ... An intensely musical person, he reacted accordingly when you started off on a wrong or false note, when he sensed affection, arbitrary attitudes. All too soon would the lion's roar be provoked. But after the thunderstorms if you were willing, there would be gentleness, helpfulness, a steady rising of hope and a new beginning.[9]

According to Anke Weihs, König could be imperious but at the same time was able to accept a fair correction or a different view. Over the years, the people who lived and worked with him experienced his unrelenting struggle, aiming to transform the traits of the lion in himself into the gentler qualities of the lamb. König did not ask for any kind of blind following but acknowledged those who had won through to an inner freedom by having gone through the eye of the needle.[10]

König was the 'spiritus rector', the spiritual head of Camphill, the undisputed leader. While members of the community addressed each other by their first names, they always called him 'Dr König'. Such a role certainly resulted in moments of loneliness, but he remained a very sociable person and his enthusiasm could have a contagious effect on those around him.[11]

A turning point in Karl König's life came at the beginning of 1955 when he was diagnosed with a serious heart condition. For weeks he hovered on the threshold between life and death and he was forced to take a break from travelling for almost a year. During this time, he received medical care from his medical assistant Hans Heinrich Engel, who later recalled how König, despite all his pain, discomfort and anxiety, had a deep insight into his own illness and everything around him.[12] However, Engel also observed that something had changed in König:

> Mildness and love pervaded his spirit-vision and knowledge more strongly and he reached the hearts in quite a different way than before … At the same time also his relationship to us, his co-workers was changing. Until then he had undoubtedly been our teacher, and for many, a father figure. But now he was becoming a friend, even a brother, and this increased with the years.[13]

In the years following his illness, König's inner development found expression in the plays he wrote for the ten days between Ascension and Whitsun.[14] In them, he tried to capture something of the disciples' mood of hope that characterised the days between their farewell to the risen Christ and the communal experience of Pentecost with the revelation of the Holy Spirit. König had already written the play *The Evening in Emmaus* for the Friday after Ascension in 1952. For König, the encounter of two disciples with the Risen Christ provided the key to future possibilities of experiencing Christ: only in retrospect and in dialogue with others were the disciples able to understand what had happened to them. Another six years passed before König wrote the two plays *Quo Vadis Domine?* and *Book of Kells* in 1958. *Quo Vadis Domine?* means 'Where are you going, Lord?' and is about Peter's experience after his threefold denial of the Lord just prior to the Crucifixion. By breaking bread together with a few women and a beggar, Peter is able to recognise:

The Sun's shining radiance rises
Up
And brightens the new day.
Now I can go to die,
For the bread
Has become life-bestowing medicine.[15]

Book of Kells, set in a round tower in Ireland, connects the Celtic spiritual tradition with Christianity.

Finally, in 1962, König wrote *The Cup of Zarathustra,* in which the mother of the disciples James and John, after a conversation with Thomas the Doubter, retrospectively recognises all kinds of connections between the events of Christ's birth and their significance for the future. Towards the end of the play, the voice of a veiled figure speaks these words:

What was sheath
Became a cup.
What was sacrifice
Became a dish.
In it shall once shine
The healing which shall work
In centuries to come.
A Grail
shall it one day be called.[16]

These plays deal with themes of awakening to deeper levels of awareness, which corresponded to König's inner experience at the time. However, they were not easily accessible and were performed only occasionally. A play for Whitsun, the Christian festival of communion permeated by the Holy Spirit, never came about.

A picture of Karl König taken by the Viennese photographer Trude Fleischmann in New York.

International activities and internal cohesion

During these later years, König went on a number of important international lecture tours, visiting several places for the first time: he went to Scandinavia and Northern Ireland in 1952, South Africa from February to May 1957, and took his first trip to the United States and Canada from July to October 1960. He visited South Africa again in 1961 and America in 1962. His last major trip, in August and September of 1965, was to Prague, Karlovy Vary and Karlstein Castle in what is now the Czech Republic, the region to which König felt a close connection.

König's travels were often linked to the planning of new communities. These were almost always based on the initiative of parents who were looking for a Camphill community to provide the special care their children needed, as well as the corresponding willingness of Camphill co-workers to carry the community impulse to new places. At that time, there was not yet a wide range of facilities geared towards people in need of special care, and many found Camphill to be an appropriate response to this situation.

In 1950, König had already been offered Thornbury Estate and the 'Sheiling' (Scottish Gaelic for 'refuge') in Ringwood, a small town in Hampshire in the south of England. Members of the founding group took over the management there.

In September 1955, the first Camphill village community was founded in Botton in Yorkshire in the north of England. For König, this foundation represented the realisation of his desire for a pastoral-medical community, which he had nurtured since the early 1930s when the Eisenach Free School for Social Work had been founded. This was made possible by Peter Roth, who, as a priest of the Christian Community, was able to realise the idea of forming a congregation within the newly founded settlement at Botton.[17] Camphill Village Botton became a model for the creation of other social therapeutic communities for adults within the Camphill movement.

In 1958, Brachenreuthe, a residential special school near Überlingen on Lake Constance, became the first Camphill centre in Germany, followed in 1964 by Föhrenbühl School.

Communities were also founded in Switzerland, Ireland, the Netherlands, Scandinavia, the United States and South Africa. Today there are over one hundred Camphill centres worldwide.

As new Camphill communities were being founded further and further afield, regular international conferences and meetings were established to maintain contact and raise awareness of the Camphill community impulse that united everyone. When people were outwardly separated from each other, inner closeness and dedication to a common spiritual content became all the more important.

The history of the Knights Templar in the vicinity of Camphill in Aberdeen drew König's attention to Rudolf Steiner's remarks on their history and significance. He chose the following paragraph from a lecture given by Rudolf Steiner on September 25, 1916 (interestingly enough on König's fourteenth birthday), as a guiding thought for the members of the Camphill Community:

> A longing for the full Christianisation of the treasures of wisdom concerning the cosmos and earthly evolution gradually broke through – a longing for the full Christianisation of earthly life so that suffering, pain and grief appear as the earth's cross, which then finds its comfort, its elevation, its salvation in the rose symbol of the crucifix. In human beings thus inspired, in whom lived on what was thought to have been destroyed with the burning of the Templars, there repeatedly lived the ideal that in place of what brings strife and quarrels something must appear that can bring good to earth; and this good may be pictured in the symbol of the cross in conjunction with the roses.[18]

The move to Central Europe

On September 27, 1962, on the occasion of Karl König's sixtieth birthday, Camphill Hall was opened in Aberdeen. König's friends compiled a book of his poetry and prose called *Wanderer im Morgenrot* (The Wanderer at Dawn), which they presented to him at the celebration. König now had an ideal location for his lectures in Scotland, but he spent more and more time on the Continent.

König's ideas were very well received in German-speaking countries, with hundreds of people attending his lectures in major cities. Gottfried Husemann, a Christian Community priest, reported on a lecture König gave in April 1963 on the then topical subject of thalidomide and the treatment of affected children. This took place in the Liederhalle, Stuttgart's concert and conference venue:

> It was overcrowded and there were boisterous scenes outside the front door. Dr König avoided becoming abusive in any way, neither against the pharmaceutical industry nor against the practice of doctors ... The warm-hearted and calmly informative nature of his presentation very soon won over the hundreds of listeners ... The way Dr König spoke about the little child was exemplary. He aroused immediate sympathy ... Furthermore, Karl König was able to make an essential contribution to the question: how should such children be treated? The most important thing is that, as far as limb stumps are still present, they are constantly stimulated to move, that they are constantly trained.[19]

König was also keen to establish more Camphill communities in Central Europe. This led to his decision to move to the Camphill school community in Brachenreuthe near Überlingen and make his new home there. His rooms in Camphill House in Aberdeen were neveretheless to remain available to him.

König and Alix Roth left Scotland on Sunday February 20, 1964, in sleet and fog. They travelled by train overnight to London where they visited König's mother, Bertha, who had moved to a Jewish retirement home. He noted in his diary for February 21, 1964: 'Then to grandmother [meaning his mother who was a grandmother]; she is well and reads to me from her biography; it is very moving.'[20]

At lunchtime, they travelled by plane to Zurich, where they were picked up for the hour-long drive to Überlingen:

> We had a very friendly journey to Brachenreuthe. There are Hans, Susi and Stella [Hans and Susanne Müller-Wiedemann (née Lissau) with daughter Stella] and it is a joyful welcome. Dinner with them all.[21]

And then the next morning, February 22:

> It's a bright day outside. The mountains shine across the lake and the sun is shining. The magic of this country takes hold of us again and we are grateful to be able to live here in the Birkenhaus.[22]

From Brachenreuthe there was a marvellous view of Lake Constance and the Swiss Alps. For König, this was a return to Central Europe where the Christian stream of the Iro-Scottish monks around St Columba the Elder and St Gallus had left clear traces everywhere: above all the monastery in St Gallen with its famous abbey library, and the island of Reichenau with its surviving church and monastery complexes. On this Shrove Tuesday, he dictated a few letters, briefly attended the carnival party with the children at the house, and then travelled into the countryside with Alix Roth: 'It's early spring and we'll go for a little walk by the lake.'[23]

On this very first day, König dealt with financial matters relating to the forthcoming foundation of Lehenhof village community in the Deggenhauser Valley, just over 7 miles (12 kilometres) away. The following day, he and Alix Roth visited the manor house in Bruckfelden, a few miles away, which had been converted into a branch of Brachenreuthe. Just a few miles further uphill, towards Heiligenberg, the official opening of Föhrenbühl residential school was imminent. Hans Heinrich Engel, who had been looking after König since his serious illness, came to visit at midday. König was looking forward to co-operating with his medical colleagues in this area. Above all, however, he wanted to devote his energies to building up the Central-European Camphill region.

Vienna

As König grew older, he became increasingly aware of the formative influence of his childhood in Vienna. He described this impressively in his memoirs, especially in contrast to Aberdeen as a Scottish harbour city, which had become a second home to him during his exile. He wove an intellectual and cultural history of Vienna into the short biographies of several nineteenth-century personalities that later appeared the book *At the Threshold of the Modern Age*. In 1963, König undertook a longer trip to Vienna, giving lectures and courses on the theory of the senses – the theme he had lectured about in January and February of 1938 before his escape.[24]

At the first stop on this journey on October 10, 1963, König noted in his diary:

> We get off the train in Salzburg in the evening and can walk through the alleyways for a while, past the houses and fountains, and everything is familiar, is 'at home', is true home.

He then wrote about Vienna on October 12:

> The sun is shining in the morning: the sky is blue and the whole magic of the city of Vienna is awake and visible. I feel full of pain and age. It is as it has always been; hardly anything seems to have changed, despite the new houses. It's just like another fashion. But the city that wears it has remained the same.

And on October 13:

> The weather is fine again in the morning. I walk through Votivpark with Alix and it is Sunday morning in Vienna.

On the following evenings he gave lectures on the theory of the senses. On October 17, he wrote:

> and then a walk through the town. It is like an enchantment ... Because it was home and has become home again so strongly, it envelops us completely.

A visit to St Stephen's Cathedral followed on Sunday 20 October:

Karl König and Alix Roth in Vienna in 1963.

> Then in St Stephen's Church, and that is a truly overwhelming impression that brings tears to my eyes. The power of Catholicism and the devotion of so many people to the sacrament is unique.[25]

Interest in Karl König was immense and he was received everywhere with enthusiasm. As a result, he promised to visit the following year.

He then travelled on to Linz to the Adalbert Stifter Archive, then to Munich for lectures, consultations with children and conversations with doctors. He also gave a filmed interviewed for a television report. Another highlight of the trip took place on Sunday, October 27 when he was awarded the gold medal of the Tutzing Star by the local branch of the international Star of Humanity, founded in 1954.[26]

This was followed by more visits with a packed schedule, including a public lecture in the large hall of the Urania in Berlin, a public lecture in Hamburg with over 1,100 people, and others in Bremen, Bochum and Cologne,

Karl König receives the gold medal of the Tutzing Star.

where he was interviewed on the radio. Then it was back to Scotland via London with stops in the various English Camphill communities.[27]

The following October 1964, König was once again able to spend several days in Vienna, the city of his early formative years. This time, he gave lectures on the subject of 'eternal childhood'.[28] In them, he described a quality of being a child that does not end at a certain point, but which can be preserved throughout life. The three lectures dealt with a brief cultural history of child anthropology and the child as the archetype of the human being in philosophy and pedagogy, with special reference to the beginnings of psychology in Vienna. These lectures showed that König was well informed about current research findings – such as those of the Vienna-born American René Spitz on childhood psychology, or the latest sociological studies on changing family forms – and was able to use them to support his presentations.

The silent stream

One topic that preoccupied Karl König during the last months of his life, and which he spoke about repeatedly on various occasions, was the Gate of the Sun and the Gate of the Moon, or the gate of life and the gate of death.[29] A small but interesting remark in his diary on March 25, 1965, exactly one year and two days before his death, shows his conscious way of dealing with the approaching end of his life, like an observer from outside:

> Up very early to go to the dentist. Last night I woke up twice and both times there was a piece of tooth on my tongue. In the morning I felt it was a sign that my body would soon be rejected like this tooth. Now it's going to be pulled.[30]

Nevertheless, he was still full of plans, especially for expanding the work in Eastern Europe: there were plans to work with doctors in what was then Czechoslovakia and in East Germany.[31]

On his last birthday, September 25, 1965, König opened Lehenhof, the first Camphill village community in Germany. In his speech, he drew on thoughts from his opening address at Whitsun 1939 in Kirkton House. While the hope and intention at that time had been to turn the spirit of Central Europe into a reality in Scotland, at Lehenhof he spoke of two great currents in the history of humankind:

> The one is the mighty stream which creates and forms, which, so to speak, brings forth and engenders everything that comes and goes in human cultures. Beside it flows a stream which one can perhaps call … the stream of silence. It is not loud; it sometimes works in secret; it does not want to fight; it does not want to be busy; it does not want to build. It wants to care, to protect, to listen and to affirm itself and its surroundings: I move my hands in the hand of God; I lead my life under the guidance of the spirit; I give my being in the devotion to others.[32]

König then described how the Iro-Scottish monks, especially Columba and Gallus, had worked at Lake Constance and influenced people in Central Europe many centuries later, such as pastor Oberlin from Alsace, poet Matthias Claudius, as well as Count Zinzendorf. König also characterised Lehenhof as a place of those who work in silence:

> If at any time in the year we open the gates and become loud, we must – so to speak – ask to be forgiven. But we shall do so gladly, because we know that many a person who comes to us takes with him a seed of silence. And in this way the world becomes a different place for him. Dear friends, it is already the case that human weakness

> … calls upon the other to awaken in himself forces of compassion which otherwise dream and sleep but do not become roused … For it is indeed true that those whom we regarded as the last are actually those who will become the first … Allow us to hope that this will gradually become a reality; that is, that the good can begin to work in this place in the name of Christ.'[33]

In the following weeks and months Karl König took up once again the question of his Jewish destiny in a lecture cycle he gave at Lake Constance. He had already spoken about this a few years earlier in Scotland. His life-long interest in embryology stood once more at the centre of lectures in Freiburg, and a last visit to Dornach also became possible. He completed the essay 'The Purpose and Value of Curative-Educational Work', in which he not only looked back on the history of curative education, but also developed a vision for its future in which it would have to take on the 'global task to help counteract the "threat to the individual person" which has arisen everywhere'.[34] The basis for this, he said, is 'the encounter of a self with another self'.[35]

Karl König died in hospital in Überlingen on March 27, 1966.

Acknowledgements

My thanks go to Richard Steel and Anne Weise of the Karl König Institute and Archive for their support.

The English edition of this book was made possible by donations from the Camphill Foundation UK and Camphill Village Newton Dee.

Notes

KKA refers to items held by the Karl König Archive.

Epigraph

1. König, *The Child with Special Needs,* p. 42.

Introduction: The Significance of Vienna for Karl König

1. König and Selg, *Karl König: My Task,* p.12.
2. See König, *At the Threshold of the Modern Age,* p. 58.
3. *Heurigen* wine refers to young wine made from the latest harvest. It was typically served until the following year's St Martin's Day (November 11), after which it was considered old wine. They were often sold in traditional wine taverns, or *Heurigers.*
4. König, *At the Threshold of the Modern Age,* p. 308.
5. The interdenominational law of May 25, 1868, recognised the legal equality of Vienna's Jews. This included allowing them entry to higher educational institutions, which meant their professional prospects were no longer restricted to trade and finance.
6. König, *At the Threshhold of the Modern Age,* p.207.
7. Ita Wegman (1876–1943) was a physician and member of the Founding Board of the General Anthroposophical Society. She was the first head of the Medical Section of the School of Spiritual Science at the Goetheanum in Dornach.
8. See Anne Weise, 'I Had Found My Home…', in the *Karl König Institute Newsletter,* no. 27, Summer 2022.
9. Emmichoven, *Wer war Ita Wegman?* pp. 227f.
10. Rudolf Steiner coined the term *seelenpflegebedürftig* as a substitute for the term 'pathological' when he was consulted about the leaflet announcing the opening of the first anthroposophical institute for curative education in Jena, Germany.
11. This expression first appeared in the title of a book called *Die Freigabe der Vernichtung Lebensunwerten Lebens* [Allowing the destruction of

life unworthy of life] by the jurist Karl Binding and the psychiatrist Alfred Hoche, two professors from the University of Freiburg. The term initially referred to people who were brain damaged, intellectually disabled or mentally ill in some way, and whom the authors felt it was justifiable to kill. Later, the term was widened to include those considered racially impure or inferior according to Nazi ideology.

12. Werner, *Anthroposophen in der Zeit des Nationalsozialismus,* pp. 1f.
13. Flügge, *Stadt ohne Seele,* pp. 211f..
14. Ibid., p. 42.
15. Flügge, *Stadt ohne Seele,* pp. 422f.
16. König and Selg, *Karl König: My Task,* pp. 11f.
17. Letter to Margit Engel dated May 16,1954. From the Karl König Archive.
18. König, diary entry of Oct 18, 1963. From the Karl König Archive.

1. Childhood and Youth (1902–20)

1. König, *At the Threshold of the Modern Age,* p. 208.
2. Bertha König spent the last years of her life in the Heinrich Stahl House in London, a German-speaking old people's home for Jewish refugees founded in 1962. Here she had the opportunity to write her memoirs, which she had been encouraged to do years before by her son and his wife.
3. See Anne Weise, 'Karl König's Ancestors: Forensic Archiving', in the *Karl König Institute Newsletter,* no. 16, Winter 2016/17.
4. König, Bertha, *Recollections of My Life,* pp. 8f.
5. König, diary entry of July 5, 1918.
6. Ibid.
7. See Regine Bruhn, 'Karl König´s Vienna: Experiences in the Prater', in the *Karl König Institute Newsletter,* no. 20, Winter 2018/19.
8. König, Bertha, *Recollections of My Life,* p. 24.
9. Ibid.
10. The care home for the poor was located at Im Werd 19, in the 2nd district of Leopoldstadt, very close to the König's family flat. The building still exists, although the inscription and figures have since been removed. Today it houses workshops for people with special needs, Jugend am Werk (Youth at Work). See John Baum, 'The Mystery of a Lost Building – Another Biographic Riddle Solved!', in the *Karl König Institute Newsletter,* no. 12, Winter 2014.
11. König, Bertha, *Recollections of My Life,* p. 25.
12. König, diary entry of July 5, 1918.
13. König, Bertha, *Recollections of My Life,* p. 24.
14. König and Selg, *Karl König: My Task,* p.17.

15. König, diary entry of July 5, 1918.
16. König, Bertha, *Recollections of My Life,* p. 25.
17. Ibid., p. 26.
18. Ibid., p. 34.
19. Ibid., p. 26.
20. König and Selg, *Karl König: My Task,* p. 17.
21. König, Bertha, *Recollections of My Life,* pp. 28f.
22. This friendship is described in more detail in Anne Weise, *Alfred Bergel: Sketches of a Forgotten Life.*
23. König, diary entry of July 6, 1918.
24. See Regine Bruhn, 'Karl König's Vienna: Experiences in the Prater', the *Karl König Institute Newsletter,* no. 20, Winter 2018–19.
25. See König, *Stories, Poems and Meditations.*
26. König, diary entry of Aug 1918, 'On art and literature in my life so far'. König occasionally wrote entries in his diary summarising his experiences over several days or a period of time. These were sometimes recorded with a range of dates (for example, see note 37 below) or, as in this case, no specific date at all.
27. Ibid.
28. König, diary entry of Sep 4, 1918.
29. König and Selg, *Karl König: My Task,* p. 17.
30. König, diary entry of July 12,1918.
31. König, diary entry for Sep 3, 1918.
32. König, diary entry for Sep 11, 1918.
33. Ibid.
34. König, diary entry for Sep 22, 1918.
35. König, diary entry for Jan 6, 1919.
36. König, diary entry for Christmas, 1919.
37. König, diary entry for April 12–16, 1919.
38. König, diary entry for May 1920.
39. König, diary entry for Feb 24, 1919.
40. König, diary entry for July 1, 1918.
41. Poem of June 8, 1917 (KKA).
42. König, diary entry for August 21, 1919.
43. König, diary entry for Nov 25, 1919.
44. König, diary entry for Jan 7, 1920.
45. König and Selg, *Karl König: My Task,* p. 18.
46. König, diary entry for Feb 24, 1919.

2. Higher Education and Training (1920–27)

1. König, diary entry for Sep 26, 1920.
2. König and Selg, *Karl König: My Task,* p. 19.
3. König, Bertha, *Recollections of My Life,* p. 31.

4. In a letter from Emil Fröschels to Godhard Husemann in 1971, Fröschels described his personal acquaintance with Rudolf Steiner and that he had mentioned him at that time in his lectures 'The Concept of Free Will in Psychotherapy' and 'The Problem of Free Will in Medicine'. It is therefore possible that König came into contact with anthroposophical thoughts at that time. See Richard Steel, 'Surprise Arrivals of Letters', in the *Karl König Institute Newsletter,* no. 21, Summer 2019.
5. Rudolf Steiner made some remarks on the constitution of the 'clubfoot' in connection with Lord Byron and his geometry teacher in the lectures he gave on karmic relationships. See Steiner, *Karmic Relationships,* vol. 1, pp. 200–204.
6. The term *Wandervogel* refers to the youth movement that emerged in 1896, which was inspired by the ideas of Romanticism and promoted folk culture and outdoor activities. This gave rise to the youth movement of the first decades of the twentieth century, from which, among other things, reform pedagogy, naturism and impulses for life reform emerged.
7. König diary entry for April 23, 1924.
8. Ibid.
9. König, diary entry for Jan 28, 1925.
10. Ibid.
11. Ibid.
12. Ibid.
13. Quoted according to Anne Weise, 'I Had Found a Home…', in the *Karl König Institute Newsletter,* no. 27, Summer 2022.
14. König and Selg, *Karl König: My Task,* pp. 21f.
15. Homeopathic solutions represent a range of decimal potencies whereby the original substance is diluted one part to nine parts solvent at each stage. So, for D1, one part of the original substance is diluted in nine parts solvent, giving a 1:10 dilution. For D2, the D1 solution is diluted again by a ratio of 1:10, resulting in a 1:100 dilution of the original substance. For D30 solution this process is repeated thirty times.
16. König and Selg, *Karl König: My Task,* p. 23.
17. König, diary entry for Oct 15, 1927.
18. One such opportunity had been the East–West Congress, held in Vienna in June 1922. At the time it was the largest public congress of the Anthroposophical Society and had come about due to Steiner's wish to achieve a greater spiritual understanding between East and West. König turned down an invitation to attend, deciding instead to focus on his studies. König and Selg, *Karl König: My Task,* p. 21. See: https://goetheanum.ch/en/news/ost-west-kongress-2022.
19. König, *The Spirit of Camphill,* p. 48.

20. König, Bertha, *Recollections of My Life,* p. 34.
21. Concerning questions surrounding the accuracy of this date see John Baum, 'Rudolf Steiner`s Sister and Karl König`s Meeting with Ita Wegman', in the *Karl König Institute Newsletter,* no. 9, Summer 2013.
22. König and Selg, *Karl König: My Task,* p. 30. The Silesian Eulengebirge is a mountain range in the Central Sudetes of south-western Poland, known for its dense forests and hiking trails popular with nature lovers.
23. Now modern-day Piława Górna in south-western Poland.
24. Moravian Brotherhood. It originated in the ideas of the Bohemian priest Jan Hus, who was burnt at the stake as a heretic in Constance in 1415.
25. For a more detailed account of Tilla Maasberg's life, see Margarete von Freeden 'Tilla König', in Bock, *The Builders of Camphill,* pp. 53–62.
26. König and Selg, *Karl König: My Task,* pp. 27f.
27. See Regine Bruhn, 'The Origin and History of the Advent Garden', in the *Karl König Institute Newsletter,* no. 24, Winter 2020.
28. See König, *The Spirit of Camphill,* pp. 50f.
29. König and Selg, *Karl König: My Task,* p. 28.
30. Ibid., p. 29.
31. Letter from the archive of the Ita Wegman Institute. Quoted by Anne Weise in 'I Had Found My Home…', in the *Karl König Institute Newsletter,* no. 27, Summer 2022.
32. See Steiner, *Education for Special Needs.*
33. Letter from the archive of the Ita Wegman Institute. Quoted by Anne Weise in 'I Had Found My Home…', in the *Karl König Institute Newsletter,* no. 27, Summer 2022.
34. König and Selg, *Karl König: My Task,* p. 34.
35. See Anne Weise, 'I Had Found My Home…', in the *Karl König Institute Newsletter,* no. 27, Summer 2022. This may also be the origin of Marie Steiner's increasing rejection of Karl König, which finally led to König's expulsion from the Anthroposophical Society in 1935.

3. The Years in Silesia (1928–35)

1. König and Selg, *Karl König: My Task,* pp. 31f.
2. Ibid., pp. 32f.
3. See Steiner, *Agricultural Course.*
4. König and Selg, *Karl König: My Task,* p. 34.
5. König, *The Spirit of Camphill,* p. 55.
6. Ibid.
7. A few years later, in August 1940, Gross-Rosen concentration camp, a subcamp of Sachsenhausen, was built through forced labour

next to the railway line from Jauer to Striegau, just over 4 miles (7 kilometres) from Pilgramshain and 37 miles (60 kilometres) south-west of Breslau. Between 1940 and 1945, 130,000 people were imprisoned there of whom approximately 40,000 were murdered. See Werner, *Anthroposophen in der Zeit des Nationalsozialismus,* p. 351.

8. König, Bertha, *Recollections of My Life,* pp. 34f.
9. See von Freeden, in Bock, *The Builders of Camphill,* p. 55.
10. König and Selg, *Karl König: My Task,* p. 12.
11. König's baptismal certificate is kept in the Karl König Archive.
12. König, Bertha, *Recollections of My Life,* pp. 35f.
13. Pilgramshain is about 186 miles (300 kilometres) north of Vienna; Arlesheim, on the other hand, is 405 miles (650 kilometres) west of Vienna.
14. König, Bertha, *Recollections of My Life,* p. 36.
15. Ibid., p. 37.
16. Bertha König is referring here as well to Tilla as her daughter-in-law, Karl König being an only child.
17. König, Bertha, *Recollections of My Life,* pp. 36f.
18. See von Freeden, in Bock, *The Builders of Camphill,* p. 55.
19. See Šárka Klímová, 'Karl König in Bohemia', in the *Karl König Institute Newsletter,* no. 17, Summer 2017.
20. Selg, *Ita Wegman and Karl König,* p. 207.
21. These liturgical celebrations held by lay people were the Sunday Service for children (7–14 years); the Youth Service (14–16 years) and the Offering Service (16 years and older). See Michaela Glöckler, 'Biographie Ita Wegman' at https://dokumentationen.kulturimpuls.org/biografien/756.
22. Selg, *Ita Wegman and Karl König,* p.10.
23. Quoted according to Frank Hörtreiter, 'Fundstellen zu Karl König aus dem Priesterrundbrief' [References to Karl König from the priests' circular letter]. Part of a compilation for the Karl König Archive.
24. See Regine Bruhn, 'The Free School of Social Work in Eisenach', in the *Karl König Institute Newsletter,* no. 21, Summer 2019.
25. Quoted according to Frank Hörtreiter, 'Fundstellen zu Karl König aus dem Priesterrundbrief' [References to Karl König from the priests' circular letter]. Part of a compilation for the Karl König Archive.
26. Ibid.
27. See Regine Bruhn, 'The Free School of Social Work in Eisenach', in the *Karl König Institute Newsletter,* no. 21, Summer 2019.
28. König, Bertha, *Recollections of My Life,* p. 37.
29. The measures of this law followed the so-called 'eugenics', a 'hereditary health doctrine', and ranged from forced sterilisation to euthanasia: In the following years, there was cynical talk of 'mercy killing'; in fact, several thousand people were murdered through

medication, food deprivation, torturous medical tests and the use of poison gas. There were many protests against this 'euthanasia order' – officially Adolf Hitler revoked it in 1941, but the deprivation of necessary nutritional components, such as fat, continued in many places. An estimated 200,000 people fell victim to this killing by the end of the war.

30. Werner, *Anthroposophen in der Zeit des Nationalsozialismus,* pp. 1f.
31. Among others, Ita Wegman was friends with Dame Florence Simpson, who had contacts in the British Royal Family, and with Kalmia Bittleston, the niece of Lord Halifax, an influential Conservative politician who for a time was British Foreign Secretary.
32. Selg, *Ita Wegman and Karl König,* p. 47.
33. Ibid., p. 57 and footnotes 65–67, pp. 248f. See also Anne Weise 'I Had Found My Home…', in the *Karl König Institute Newsletter,* no. 27, Summer 2022.
34. Selg, Ita Wegman and Karl Konig, pp. 59f.
35. For the exact wording of the ban by the Prussian Secret State Police in Berlin, see Werner, *Anthroposophen in der Zeit des Nationalsozialismus,* p.76.
36. Werner, *Anthroposophen in der Zeit des Nationalsozialismus,* p. 181.
37. König, *The Spirit of Camphill,* pp. 59f.
38. König, Bertha, *Recollections of My Life,* p. 31.
39. See Šárka Klímová, 'Karl König in Bohemia', in the *Karl König Institute Newsletter,* no. 17, Summer 2017.
40. König, *At the Threshold of the Modern Age,* p. 377.
41. König, *Stories, Poems and Meditations*, pp. 220f.
42. Karl König was called 'Markus' by his wife, Tilla, throughout his life. The origin of this is unknown, but possibly it refers to 'Brother Markus' in Goethe's poem 'The Mysteries'. See Rudolf Steiner, *Inner Impulses of Evolution,* lecture of Sep 25, 1916.
43. König, *Stories, Poems and Meditations*, pp. 221f.
44. Mann, *Wallenstein,* pp. 581ff.
45. The threefold social order, or social threefolding, refers to a social structure in which social processes are organised in three separate areas in accordance with the three ideals of the French Revolution: freedom in spiritual life, equality in legal life and brotherhood in economic life. See Rudolf Steiner, *Towards Social Renewal.*

4. The Viennese Years and Emigration (1936–38)

1. Moritz Gerstler left Germany in 1933 and returned to Vienna, where he died of tuberculosis in an institution in 1937.
2. Bock, *The Builders of Camphill,* p. 71.
3. König and Selg, *Karl König: My Task,* p. 40.

4. Bock, *The Builders of Camphill,* p. 70.
5. Ibid.
6. Schauder met König in August 1933 and shortly after spent a month at Pilgramshain. See Schauder, *Vienna My Home,* pp.78f.
7. Hanna Lissau was a curative teacher who, after her training in Arlesheim, joined a curative education initiative led by Vala Bérence in France. After the German occupation of France, she was warned by the police that she would be arrested in the next few days and was advised to flee across the Pyrenees. She told staff at the home that she had never really felt part of Judaism but now wanted to help the Jews. She was prepared when the police arrived. From the Drancy collection camp near Paris, she was deported to Auschwitz on September 9, 1942, where she was murdered on October 14. See John Baum, 'The Youth Group in Vienna', in Bock, *The Builders of Camphill,* p. 20f.
8. Bock, *The Builders of Camphill,* pp.26f.
9. Ibid., pp. 11f.
10. König, *The Spirit of Camphill,* pp. 62f.
11. For a long time Oberufer was a mainly German-speaking village centred around a ferry station on the so-called 'Grosse Schütt', the largest river island in Europe that sits between the Danube, the Small Danube and the Waag and which actually consists of 500 small islets. The Oberufer Christmas plays are regularly performed in Waldorf schools and many other anthroposophical institutions.
12. König and Selg, *Karl König: My Task,* p. 41.
13. See Rudolf Steiner, Becoming the Archangel Michael's Companion.
14. Selg, *Ita Wegman and Karl König,* p.65.
15. König, *The Spirit of Camphill,* p. 61.
16. Flügge, *Stadt ohne Seele,* p.42: 'In the 1920s anti-Semitic incidents increased, such as the attack on the Anatomical Institute of the University of Vienna. Thugs paraded through the streets of Leopoldstadt. This district was almost considered an Eastern European Stetl in the big city, popularly called "Mazzeinsel", but even here no more than 30 percent of the inhabitants were Jews. In 1938 there were about 170,000 Jews living in Vienna; in 1945 there were still 6,000. More than 65,000 Viennese Jews perished in the Holocaust.'
17. König, Bertha, *Recollections of My Life,* p. 39.
18. König and Selg, *Karl König: My Task,* p. 42.
19. Selg, *Ita Wegman and Karl König,* p. 203.
20. König and Selg, *Karl König: My Task,* p. 43.
21. Ibid., pp. 134f.
22. Ibid., pp. 43f.

23. Ibid., p. 44.
24. As quoted in König and Selg, *Karl König: My Task,* pp. 43f. See also, Steiner, *Becoming the Archangel Michael's Companion,* lecture of Oct 15, 1922, pp. 152 and 156.
25. König, *The Spirit of Camphill,* p. 141.
26. Schauder, *Vienna My Home,* pp. 87f.
27. Ibid., pp .89f.
28. König and Selg, *Karl König: My Task,* p. 46.
29. Ibid.
30. König, Bertha, *Recollections of My Life,* p. 40.
31. Ibid., p. 40.
32. Bock, *The Builders of Camphill,* p. 238.
33. Ibid., p. 72.
34. Ibid., p. 73.
35. König and Selg, *Karl König: My Task,* p. 49.
36. Lucia de Viti de Marco was the daughter of the Italian economist and liberal democratic politician Antonio de Viti de Marco. Several members of the family belonged to König's group of patients.
37. König, Bertha, *Recollections of My Life,* pp. 39f.
38. König and Selg, *Karl König: My Task,* p. 49.
39. König, Bertha, *Recollections of My Life,* p. 40.
40. Emmichoven, *Wer war Ita Wegman?* p. 227.
41. Selg, *Ita Wegman and Karl König,* p. 68. Dame Florence Simpson was the founder of the Royal Women's Volunteer Service of the British Army, known as 'Queen Mary's Army Auxiliary Corps', and was a friend of Queen Mary, the wife of King George V. Dame Florence had invited Ita Wegman on several summer trips. See Emmichoven, *Wer war Ita Wegman?* pp. 227f.
42. The letter is held in the Karl König Archive.
43. On September 29, 1938, the Munich Agreement was signed allowing the German Wehrmacht to invade the Sudetenland, which until then had been controlled by Czechoslovakia.
44. König, *The Spirit of Camphill,* pp. 146f.
45. Ibid., p. 155.
46. Selg, *Ita Wegman and Karl König,* pp. 200f.
47. The letter is held in the Karl König Archive.
48. König, *Plays for the Festivals of the Year,* pp. 62f.
49. König, *The Spirit of Camphill,* pp. 90f.
50. Ibid., p. 92.
51. König's mother, Bertha, describes in her memoirs how Tilla's departure from Germany was made difficult by officials not wanting her to take her two boys who could serve as future members of the Hitler Youth. Tilla is said to have pulled a knife,

claiming that the boys would only stay behind 'over her dead body'. Tilla and her children were allowed to leave the country. See Bertha König, *Recollections of My Life,* p.41.

52. See König, Bertha, *Recollections of My Life,* pp. 41f.

5. Arrival in Scotland (1938–40)

1. Between 1935 and 1941 alone, the Quaker Relief Service helped more than 1,100 people flee the Nazis.
2. König, *Camphill. Ursprung und Ziele einer Bewegung,* p.74.
3. Cecil Harwood was a Waldorf teacher and, from 1937 to 1974, the General Secretary of the Anthroposophical Society in Great Britain. During his studies at Oxford University he was a member of the Inklings, a literary circle centred around C.S. Lewis and J.R.R. Tolkien, which also included Harwood's school friend Owen Barfield. See Bock, *The Builders of Camphill,* p. 7.
4. König, *The Spirit of Camphill,* p. 146.
5. Bock, *The Builders of Camphill,* pp. 238f.
6. 'Fräulein Lissau' was Susanne Lissau, later Müller-Wiedemann. In a letter to Ita Wegman on April 14, 1940, Karl König expressed his disappointment that she was still not available, as Scotland desperately needed a eurythmy therapist and musician. Susanne Lissau was able to stay in Switzerland during the war and only came later to Camphill in Scotland. See Selg, *Ita Wegman and Karl König,* pp. 202f.
7. Selg, *Ita Wegman and Karl König,* p. 202.
8. Bock, *The Builders of Camphill,* p. 291.
9. Schauder, *Vienna My Home,* p. 104.
10. König, *The Spirit of Camphill,* p. 158.
11. Ibid., p. 191.
12. Ibid., p. 166
13. Weihs, 'Fragments from the Story of Camphill 1939–1940', in König, *The Spirit of Camphill,* p.186.
14. Weise, 'Camphill: Haven for Jewish Refugees', in the *Karl König Institute Newsletter,* no. 18, Winter 2017/18. Peter Bergel was no relation of Karl König's childhood friend Alfred Bergel.
15. Ibid.
16. Kalmia Bittleston (1909–89) was born in South Africa and ordained a priest in The Christian Community by Alfred Heidenreich in October 1944, together with Peter Roth, among others. She was a sister of the priest Adam Bittleston and niece of Lord Halifax, then British Foreign Secretary. See Hörtreiter, *Die Christengemeinschaft im Nationalsozialismus,* p. 69, p. 224 and p. 375.
17. See John Baum, 'Kalmia Bittleston and the Opening of Kirkton

House', in the *Karl König Institute Newsletter,* no. 11, Summer 2014.

18. What König probably meant here is 'British' or 'English-speaking' rather than just 'English'. Only slowly did he become aware that there are major historical, cultural and legal differences between the countries of the United Kingdom in addition to their similarities.
19. König, *The Spirit of Camphill,* p. 16.
20. König and Selg, *Karl König: My Task,* pp. 144f.
21. König and Selg, *Karl König: My Task,* pp. 191f.
22. Selg, *Ita Wegman and Karl König,* p. 205.
23. Ibid., pp. 84f.
24. König, *The Spirit of Camphill,* p. 159.
25. Ibid., pp. 205f.
26. Ibid., pp. 169f.
27. See Anne Weise, 'Camphill: Haven for Jewish Refugees', in the *Karl König Institute Newsletter,* no. 18, Winter 2017/18.
28. See Anne Weise, 'Woman Explores Isle of Man', in the *Karl König Institute Newsletter,* no. 8, Winter 2012.
29. Schauder, *Vienna My Home,* pp. 112f.
30. Ibid.
31. See König, *The Calendar of the Soul* and *Plays for the Festivals of the Year.*
32. König, *The Spirit of Camphill,* p. 198.
33. Ibid., p. 200.
34. König, *Camphill. Ursprung und Ziele einer Bewegung,* p.239 (author's translation).

6. Camphill: Building a Community (1941–44)

1. See Steiner, *Education for Special Needs,* lecture of July 6, 1924. One of the initiators of this Curative Education Course, Siegfried Pickert, wrote the following words of introduction in 1995 on the occasion of the 100th birthday of his colleague Franz Löffler: 'It was a festive moment when in bright sunshine on 18 June 1924 Rudolf Steiner looked across, together with us, from Lauenstein to 'Paradise', the banks of the Saale, where Goethe received essential impressions for the "Fairy Tale". Two motifs resound and shine across in particular: "One alone does not help, but he who unites with many at the right hour" and "Love does not rule, but it educates and that is more".' Girke, *Franz Löffler,* p.10.
2. The Knights Templar existed from 1119 to 1312 and were the first order to unite the ideals of aristocratic chivalry and monasticism, which had previously been strictly separated. They developed a wide range of organisational and economic activities, issued money loans and invented a type of letter of credit that was even used by their Muslim neighbours. They combined this with an advanced

form of bookkeeping and endeavoured to always carry out their extensive practical activities in accordance with their spiritual beliefs. King Philip IV of France (known as Philip the Fair) was heavily indebted to the Templars and sought to destroy them and seize their wealth. On the basis of fabricated charges of heresy, King Philip ordered the arrest of all Templars in France on Friday, October 13, 1307. Their Grand Master, Jacques de Molay, was executed in 1314.

3. Some sources give March 18, 1314, as the date Jacques de Molay was executed. Karl König's library contains a book by Ernst Sommer called *Die Templer* in which March 11, 1314 is given as the date.
4. König and Selg, *Karl König: My Task,* pp.13f.
5. König, *The Spirit of Camphill,* pp. 202f.
6. George MacLeod (1895–1991) was a clergyman in the Church of Scotland and founder of the Iona Community.
7. Selg, *Ita Wegman and Karl König,* p. 236. The letter is held in the Karl König Archive.
8. König, *The Spirit of Camphill,* pp. 172f.
9. König, *The Spirit of Camphill,* p. 204. The threefold organisation of the human organism is a central principle of anthroposophical anthropology. A distinction is made between the nervous-sensory system, the rhythmic system (heart and blood circulation) and the metabolic-limb system. It can also refer to the holistic view of the human being as body, soul and spirit or to the division of the soul forces into thinking, feeling and willing.
10. Ibid., pp.198f.
11. Ibid., p. 204.
12. The esteem in which James Downie Campbell was held in Aberdeen is illustrated by the fact that he was appointed Deputy Lieutenant of the City of Aberdeen on May 1, 1967. In this role, it was his duty to represent the city on official visits by the royal family.
13. Müller-Wiedemann, *Karl König,* p.176.
14. Bock, *The Builders of Camphill,* pp. 63 and 253f.
15. König, *Plays for the Festivals of the Year,* pp. 69f.
16. Ibid., pp. 305f.
17. Schauder, *Vienna My Home,* pp. 120f.
18. Ibid., pp. 108f.
19. Ibid., pp.124f.
20. See also, König, *Music Therapy*.
21. Schauder, *Vienna My Home,* p. 24.
22. Ibid., p. 129.
23. König, *The Spirit of Camphill,* p.151.
24. Lefébure and Schauder, *Conversations on Counselling*.
25. Werner, *Anthroposophen in der Zeit des Nationalsozialismus,* p.320.

26. Hörtreiter, *Die Christengemeinschaft im Nationalsozialismus,* pp. 97f.
27. The document can be found in the Karl König Archive. The agreement was dissolved in this form in 1948, when both movements were once again able to develop more independently of each other. See also Hörtreiter, *Die Christengemeinschaft im Nationalsozialismus,* p. 223.
28. George Adams (1894–1963), formerly George von Kaufmann was a mathematician and translator.
29. Müller-Wiedemann, *Karl König,* pp. 255f.
30. König drew further inspiration from the figure of Kaspar Hauser in a story he wrote for Christmas 1946 called *Also a Christmas Story*. Set on Christmas Eve, the narrator of the story takes a break from the busy festive preparations and goes on a walk through the landscape where the Templars once lived. Images of Scottish and Austrian landscapes are woven together in a dreamlike fashion throughout the walk until the narrator finds himself in the Land of Life and Truth. Here Kaspar Hauser has preserved a home for the eternal self of children and colleagues the narrator knew but who have recently died. Here, their future path from heaven to earth is prepared. König handed the completed story to his wife Tilla on March 11, 1947, exactly five years after the stillbirth of their child, who was now to be found, in an imaginative way, in the Land of Life and Truth watched over by Kaspar Hauser. See König, *Stories, Poems and Meditations*, pp. 239-53.
31. After 18 years, 7 months and 9 days, the intersections of the orbits of the moon and sun are once again in the same position in the zodiac.
32. See 'Thoughts on Kasper Hauser', in Selg and Steel, *Kaspar Hauser and Karl König,* pp. 83–97.
33. See Konig, *Plays for the Festivals of the Year,* pp. 285-301.
34. König, *The Spirit of Camphill,* pp. 174f. König is here referencing the lecture Steiner gave on Jan 1, 1906, called 'The Science of the Spirit and the Social Question'. See Steiner, *Reincarnation and Immortality,* pp. 195f.
35. Pietzner, *A Candle on the Hill,* pp. 97f.
36. König, *The Spirit of Camphill,* pp. 93f.
37. Ibid., p. 95.
38. In Germany also known as Herrnhuter or Herrnhuter Brüdergemeine, referring to the name of Count Zinzendorf's estate where he hosted them. It's literal meaning is 'under the care of the Lord'.
39. König, *The Spirit of Camphill,* pp. 100f.
40. Ibid., pp. 102f.
41. Ibid., p. 107.

42. Ibid., pp. 110f.
43. Ibid., pp. 114f.
44. Ibid., pp. 119f.
45. Overall, it can be observed that state regulations are having a growing influence on the organisation of everyday life and social coexistence almost everywhere, particularly in terms of strengthening the individual rights of people with support needs. Dan McKanan, Emerson Lecturer at Harvard Divinity School in the USA, explains in his studies on Camphill and other intentional communities that such changes should not be seen as a threat but as an opportunity. See McKanan, *Camphill and the Future* and *Eco-Alchemy*.

7. Developments and Transformations (1945–63)

1. König, *Plays for the Festivals of the Year,* pp. 103f.
2. Ibid., p. 146.
3. Ibid., p. 152.
4. Ibid., pp.182f.
5. Ibid., p. 195.
6. Ibid., pp. 227f.
7. Ibid., p. 98.
8. Müller-Wiedemann, *Karl König,* p.181. The manuscript of the report, dated August 14, 1948, is held in the Karl König Archive.
9. Edith Tudor-Hart, née Suschitzky (1908–73), had been active as a spy for the KGB, the Soviet intelligence agency, and was responsible for recruiting the 'Cambridge Five', a group of Cambridge students that included Kim Philby, Guy Burgess and Donald Maclean. Through peace researcher Robert Jungk, the husband of her cousin Ruth, Edith Tudor-Hart met her then lover, the Viennese chemist and nuclear scientist Engelbert Broda – the same Broda who had published Alex Baum's chemical dissertation in London without his knowledge. It is doubtful whether anyone at Camphill knew about this connection. On the connection between Alex Baum and Engelbert Broda, see Bock, *The Builders of Camphill,* p. 259.
10. Pietzner, *A Candle on the Hill,* pp. 43f.
11. The term 'entelechy' (from the Greek *entelécheia*) was coined by Aristotle and referred to the form that is realised in matter, the force within an organism that brings about its development and perfection. It is the individual spirit independent of time and space.
12. See Nauck, *We Came.*
13. König, *Plays for the Festivals of the Year,* pp. 335f.
14. Müller-Wiedemann, *Karl König,* pp. 365f.
15. Ibid., p. 366.
16. Bock, *The Builders of Camphill,* pp. 59f.

17. König, diary entry for May 2, 1954.
18. König, diary entry for May 4, 1954.
19. König, diary entry for May 5, 1954.
20. Ibid.
21. König, diary entry for May 7, 1954.
22. König, diary entry for May 8, 1954.
23. Bock, *The Builders of Camphill,* pp .61f.
24. Ibid, pp.187f.
25. See Tobis, *Thalamos.*
26. Down's syndrome is named after the pharmacist John Langdon Down, who first described the syndrome in detail in 1866. Today it is also referred to as 'trisomy 21' because of a tripling instead of doubling of chromosome 21 in each cell.
27. König and Selg, *Karl König: My Task,* pp. 136f.
28. Ibid., p. 137.
29. A chronological bibliography of his works, including updates and further information, can be found on the website of the Karl König Institute at karlkoeniginstitute.org. Books from the Karl König Archive series can also be purchased from Floris Books at florisbooks.co.uk.
30. Ernst Klee's *Euthanasie im NS-Staat,* published in 1983, and its follow-up published in 1985, *Dokumente zur Euthanasie im NS-Saat,* are considered the standard works on the subject today. His books *Auschwitz: die NS-Medizin und ihre Opfer* from 1997 and *Deutsche Medizin im Dritten Reich* were honoured with the Geschwister Scholl Prize and the Goethe Plaque awards. Another standard work of reference followed in 2003 with Klee's biographical encyclopaedia, *Das Personenlexikon zum Dritten Reich.*
31. Klee, *Das Personenlexikon zum Dritten Reich,* p. 339.
32. König, *Seeds for Social Renewal,* pp. 93f. In this context König also developed a typology for female constitutions.
33. Johann 'Hans' Friedrich Karl Asperger (1906–80) first named a disorder he called 'autistic psychopathy' in 1938. He only became internationally recognised in the 1980s when the British psychologist Lorna Wing became aware of his research and, following on from this, defined and named the syndrome after him. It was only later that it became known that Asperger had been a consultant at the Vienna Health Department during the Nazi era and had worked as an expert in a commission that was supposed to categorise children with disabilities according to their educational ability in so-called 'special schools'. The decisive factor here was the supposed ability to integrate into the so-called 'national community'. Out of 200 cases, 35 were assessed as 'hopeless cases', whereupon they were all murdered in the Viennese youth

welfare centre Am Spiegelgrund as part of the Nazi euthanasia programme. It is disputed to what extent Asperger played an active role in this and his other activities; in any case, he contributed to the legitimisation of these murders as an 'expert'. For details and background, see Sheffer, *Asperger's Children.*

34. König, diary entry for May 3, 1954.
35. König, diary entry for May 6, 1954.
36. Letter from Karl König to Margit Engel dated May 6, 1954 (KKA).
37. König, diary entry for May 10, 1954.
38. Letter from Paul Regenstreif to Karl König dated October 6, 1955 (KKA).
39. Letter from Paul Regenstreif to Karl König dated Jan 18, 1957. König's reply dated Jan 22, 1957. Both letters held by the Karl König Archive.
40. Letter from Karl König to Paul Regenstreif dated Feb 3, 1959 (KKA).
41. Letter from Karl König to Paul Regenstreif dated June 17, 1959 (KKA).
42. Letter from Paul Regenstreif to Karl König dated October 30, 1959 (KKA).
43. Letter from Karl König to Paul Regenstreif dated Nov 3, 1959 (KKA).
44. Werner Catel (1894–81) was significantly involved in the Third Reich's child euthanasia programme. Criminal proceedings against him were dropped in the early 1960s because, according to the state of knowledge at the time, it could not be proven that he had a 'hostile intent' or the motive of 'malice' in the killing of children. Selg, *Heilpädagogik oder 'Kindereuthanasie'?* p. 214.
45. Letter from Werner Catel to Karl König dated Dec 13, 1957 (KKA).
46. Nazi ideology differentiated between those children with special educational needs for whom mental development was considered possible through curative education, and those with a supposed 'emptiness of mind' or 'emotional void' (*Gemütsleere*) for whom it was deemed no help could be given. At the time, this distinction provided the criterion for eugenic measures such as sterilisation or even euthanasia.
47. Letter from Werner Catel to Karl König dated June 7, 1958, held by Karl König Archive.
48. Letter from Karl König to Werner Catel dated June 18, 1958 (KKA).
49. Selg, *Heilpädagogik oder 'Kindereuthanasie'?* p. 151.
50. Letter from Werner Catel to Karl König dated April 14, 1960 (KKA).
51. Letter from Werner Catel to Karl König dated Sep 29, 1960 (KKA).
52. König, diary entry for June 28, 1962.
53. König, diary entry for June 29, 1962.
54. König, diary entry for August 1, 1963.
55. Letter from Karl König to Fritz Götte dated July 29, 1963 (KKA).
56. Selg, *Heilpädagogik oder 'Kindereuthanasie'?* pp. 196f.
57. Ibid., pp. 210f.

8. The Last Years (1963–66)

1. König, diary entry for October 4, 1965.
2. König and Selg, *Karl König: My Task,* pp. 143f.
3. König, diary entry for May 17, 1953.
4. König, diary entry for Jan 12, 1954.
5. König, diary entry for April 20, 1954.
6. König, diary entry for June 26, 1954.
7. Pietzner, *A Candle on the Hill,* p. 25.
8. König and Selg, *Karl König: My Task,* pp. 140f.
9. Ibid., pp. 142f.
10. Ibid., pp. 146f.
11. Ibid., p. 144.
12. Ibid., pp. 153f.
13. Ibid., pp. 155f.
14. König, *Plays for the Festivals of the Year,* pp. 201–68.
15. Ibid., p. 226.
16. Ibid., p. 263.
17. Bruhn, Regine, 'The Free School for Social Work in Eisenach 1932', in Newsletter 21 of the Karl König Institute, Summer 2019.
18. Steiner, *The Knights Templar,* pp. 69f. See also, König, *The Spirit of Camphill,* pp. 11f.
19. Quoted according to Frank Hörtreiter from the 'Priesterrundbrief'. Part of a summary for the Karl König Archive, 2022.
20. König, diary entry for Feb 21, 1964.
21. Ibid.
22. König, diary entry for Feb 22, 1964.
23. Ibid.
24. König, *Die zwölf Sinne des Menschen,* p.15.
25. König, diary entries for October 10–20, 1963.
26. König, *The Spirit of Camphill,* pp. 178f.
27. König, *Die zwölf Sinne des Menschen,* p.218.
28. König, *Ewige Kindheit.*
29. See König, *Before Birth and Beyond Death.*
30. König, diary entry for March 25, 1965.
31. For König's plans for Czechoslovakia see Šárka Klímová, 'Karl König in Bohemia', in Newsletter 17 of the Karl König Institute, Summer 2017.
32. Müller-Wiedemann, *Karl König,* pp. 479f.
33. Ibid., pp .480f.
34. König, *The Child with Special Needs,* p. 42.
35. Ibid.

Bibliography

Bock, Friedwart (ed.), *The Builders of Camphill: Lives and Destinies of the Founders,* Floris Books, UK 2005.

Catel, Werner, *Grenzsituationen des Lebens. Beitrag zum Problem der begrenzten Euthanasie* [Borderline situations in life: A contribution to the problem of limited euthanasia], Glock und Lutz, Germany 1962.

Emmichoven, J.E. Zeylmans van, *Wer war Ita Wegman? Eine Dokumentation 1925–1943,* Vol. 2, Verlag am Goetheanum, Switzerland 1992 (published in English as *Who was Ita Wegman? A documentation,* Vol. 2, SteinerBooks, USA 1996.

Flügge, Manfred, *Stadt ohne Seele: Wien 1938* [A City Without a Soul: Vienna, 1938], Aufbau Verlag, Germany 2018.

Girke, Hermann, *Franz Löffler: Ein Leben für Anthroposophie und heilende Erziehung im Zeitenschicksal* [Franz Löffler: A life for anthroposophy and healing education in the context of the times], Verlag am Goetheanum, Switzerland 1995.

Hörtreiter, Frank, *Die Christengemeinschaft im Nationalsozialismus* [The Christian Community under National Socialism], Urachhaus, Gemany 2021.

Klee, Ernst, *Auschwitz: die NS-Medizin und ihre Opfer* [Auschwitz: Nazi medicine and its victims], Fischer, Germany 1997.

—, *Deutsche Medizin im Dritten Reich. Karrieren vor und nach 1945* [German medicine in the Third Reich: careers before and after 1945], Fischer, Germany 2001.

—, *Dokumente zur Euthanasie im NS-Saat* [Documents on euthanasia in the Nazi state], Fischer, Germany 1985.

—, *Euthanasie im NS-Staat: Die Vernichtung lebensunwerten Lebens* [Euthanasia in the Nazi state: the extermination of life unworthy of life], Fischer, Germany 1983.

—, *Das Personenlexikon zum Dritten Reich. Wer war was vor und nach 1945* [The biographical dictionary of the Third Reich: Who was who before and after 1945], Fischer, Germany 2005.

König, Bertha, *Recollections of My Life,* manuscript in the Karl König Archive.

König, Karl, *At the Threshold of the Modern Age: Biographies Around the Year 1861,* Floris Books, UK 2011.

—, *Before Birth and Beyond Death: The Transformation of the Human Being,* Floris Books, UK 2021.

—, *Brothers and Sisters: The Order of Birth in the Family,* Floris Books, UK 2014.

—, *The Calendar of the Soul: An Inner Journey Through the Year,* Floris Books, UK 2025.

—, *Camphill. Ursprung und Ziele einer Bewegung,* Freies Geistesleben, Germany 2019 (English published as *The Spirit of Camphill*).

—, *The Child with Special Needs: Letters and Essays on Curative Education,* Floris Books, UK 2009.

—, *Ewige Kindheit* [Eternal childhood], Camphill Verlag, Germany 1994.

—, *The First Three Years of the Child: How Children Learn to Walk, Speak and Think,* Floris Books, UK 2023.

—, *The Human Soul: Mysteries and Complexities of the Psyche,* Floris Books, UK 2025.

—, *Music Therapy: Research and Insights,* Floris Books, UK 2024.

—, *Plays for the Festivals of the Year,* Floris Books, UK 2017.

—, *Seeds for Social Renewal: The Camphill Village Conferences,* Floris Books, UK 2009.

—, *The Spirit of Camphill: Birth of a Movement,* Floris Books, UK 2018.

—, *Stories, Poems and Meditations,* Floris Books, UK 2020.

—, *Die zwölf Sinne des Menschen. Band 1: Der Kreis der zwölf Sinne und die Ich-Entwicklung* [The twelve human senses. Vol 1: the circle of the twelve senses and the development of the ego], Freies Geistesleben, Germany 2021.

König, Karl, and Selg, Peter (ed.), *Karl König: My Task,* Floris Books, UK 2008.

Lefébure, Marcus, and Schauder, Hans, *Conversations on Counselling: Between a Doctor and a Priest,* T & T Clark, UK 1990.

Mann, Golo, *Wallenstein: Sein Leben erzählt von Golo Mann* [Wallenstein: his life as told by Golo Mann], Fischer, Germany 1974.

McKanan, Dan, *Camphill and the Future: Spirituality and Disability in an Evolving Communal Movement,* University of California Press, USA 2020.

—, *Eco-Alchemy: Anthroposophy and the History and Future of Environmentalism,* University of California Press, USA 2018.

Müller-Wiedemann, Hans, *Karl König: A Central-European Biography of the Twentieth Century,* Camphill Books, UK 1996.

Nauck, Erika (ed.), *We Came: Biographic Sketches of the Twenty-Five Participants of the First Camphill Seminar in Curative Education 1949–1951,* Camphill Books, UK 2009.

Pietzner, Cornelius (ed.), *A Candle on the Hill: Images of Camphill Life,* Floris Books, UK 1990.

Schauder, Hans, *Vienna My Home,* privately printed, UK 2002.

Selg, Peter, *Heilpädagogik oder 'Kindereuthanasie'? Karl Königs Auseinandersetzung mit Werner Catel* [Special education or 'child euthanasia': Karl König's argument with Werner Catel], Ita Wegman Institut, Switzerland 2021.

Selg, Peter (ed.), *Ita Wegman and Karl König: Letters and Documents,* Floris Books, UK 2008.

Sheffer, Edith, *Asperger's Children: The Origins of Autism in Nazi Vienna,* W W Norton, UK 2018.

Selg, Peter and Steel, Richard (eds.), *Kaspar Hauser and Karl König,* Floris Books, UK 2012.

Steiner Rudolf, (CW = Collected works, GA = German Gesamtausgabe)

—, *Agriculture: Spiritual-Scientific Foundations for Agricultural Renewal* (CW327), Rudolf Steiner Press, UK 2024.

—, *Becoming the Archangel Michael's Companion: Rudolf Steiner's Challenge to the Younger Generation* (CW217), SteinerBooks, USA 2007.

—, *Education for Special Needs: The Curative Education Course* (CW317), Rudolf Steiner Press, UK 2015.

—, *Karmic Relationships – Esoteric Studies,* Vol. 1, Rudolf Steiner Press, UK 1997.

—, *The Knights Templar: The Mystery of the Warrior Monks,* Rudolf Steiner Press, UK 2007.

—, *Reincarnation and Immortality,* SteinerBooks, USA 1970.

—, *Towards Social Renewal: Rethinking the Basis of Society* (CW23), Rudolf Steiner Press, UK 1999.

Tobis, Almut, *Thalamos – Eine Heilmittelentwicklung. Myrrhe, Weihrauch, Gold und der werdende Mensch* [Thalamos – A medicinal development: myrrh, frankincense, gold, and the developing human being], Freies Geisteleben, Germany 2025.

Weise, Anne, *Alfred Bergel, Sketches of a Forgotten Life: From Vienna to Auschwitz,* Temple Lodge, UK 2021.

Werner, Uwe, *Anthroposophen in der Zeit des Nationalsozialismus (1933–1945)* [Anthroposophists during the Nazi Era (1933–1945)], De Gruyter Oldenbourg, Germany 1999.

Zeylmans van Emmichoven, J.E., see Emmichoven, J.E. Zeylmans van.

Index

Adams, George 149
advent spiral 57f
Amann, Willi 128, 133
Andreas-Lindberg, Christoph 191
Anschluss 97–101
anthroposophy 49f
Asperger, Hans 180–83

Baum, Alex 91, 118, 128, 133
Bergel, Alfred 'Fredi' 30, 34, 51
Bergel, Arnold 35
Bergel, Arthur 30
Bergel, Peter 122
Bittleston, Kalmia 123
Blau, Trude 91, 118, 123, 131
Blitz, Marie 117, 123, 131
Bock, Emil 68, 75–79
Botton Village 154, 196

Camphill 127
— annual festivals 143f
— community life 139–43, 151f
— expansion 152f
— in Central Europe 198f
—, public interest in 166f
— religious life 147f
Camphill Seminar 169
Catel, Werner 183–88
Charles IV (Emperor) 85f
Christian Community, The 49, 75, 148f
Columba, St 135f, 138
Comenius, John Amos 155f, 158

Emmichoven, Willem Zeylmans van 80
Engel, Hans Heinrich 193

Förster, Hanna 90f
Free School for Social Work 78f

Garvald 145
Gerstler, Sali 88f, 103, 117
Goethe, Johann Wolfgang von 134

Harwood, Cecil 116
Hauser, Kaspar 150f
Heidenreich, Alfred 148f
Herrnhut Brethren 56
Hitler, Adolf 79, 98f
Hütter, Bronja 91

internment 127–31

Kirkton House 110, 120–27
Knights Templar 135f, 197
Kolisko, Eugen 107–09, 122
König, Adolf Aron Ber 22f
König, Bertha (née Fischer) 24f, 66, 68f, 95, 106f, 113f
König, Karl
— and Christianity 39f, 55
— and Judaism 37f, 41f, 55
— Bar Mitzvah 32
— embryological studies 51f
— escape from Austria 105f
— expulsion from the Anthroposophical Society 81f

— health 192f
— in Brachenreuthe 199f
— in London 111f
— lecturing activities 59f, 170, 175f, 195f, 198
— marriage 68
— return to Vienna 173f, 200–04
— socialist interests 46f
— Tutzing Star award 202
König, Mathilde 'Tilla' (née Maasberg) 55f, 60f, 71f, 122, 131, 172f
Kretschmer, Ernst 180

Lazarus, Irmgard 177
Lehrs, Ernst 130, 133
Lissau, Rudi 91, 100

Macmillan, William 127
Müller-Wiedemann, Hans 170f
Müller-Wiedemann, Susanne (née Lissau) 91, 177
Murtle estate 154

Nederhoed, Ann *see* Weihs, Anke
Newton Dee 154

Owen, Robert 157f

Pietzner, Carlo 92, 117, 128, 133
Pilgramshain 64f

Rascher, Ilse 68f
Rascher, Michael 68f
Roth, Alix 92, 117, 131, 175f, 199f
Roth, Ann *see* Weihs, Anke
Roth, Peter 92, 116, 120f, 133, 149, 154

Samojé, Rudi 122, 128
Schauder, Hans 90f, 99f, 118f, 125, 128f, 133
— departs Camphill 144–47
Schauder, Lisl *see* Schwalb, Elisabeth 'Lisl'
Schwalb, Elisabeth 'Lisl' 91, 117f, 120, 131
Sonnenhof 57f
Stein, Walter Johannes 81
Steiner, Marie 61, 76
Steiner, Rudolf 49, 53f, 57f, 64, 93f, 134, 157, 197
Strohschein, Albrecht 61
Sucher, Willi 130, 133, 150

therapeutic research 176f
Tudor-Hart, Edith 167

Vienna 10f,

Waldhaus 56, 62f
Wallenstein, Albrecht von 86f
Wegman, Ita 14, 53f, 57, 59f, 65, 72f, 80f, 93f, 96, 107f, 110, 117f, 125f, 150
Weihs, Anke 97, 116f, 122, 124f, 131f, 137f, 140f, 176f, 189f
Weihs, Thomas 92, 118, 133, 154
Weissberg, Eduard 'Edi' 90f

Zinzendorf, Nikolaus Count von 141, 156–8

Karl König Archive volumes

1 Karl König: My Task: Autobiography and Biographies
2 Karl König's Path into Anthroposophy: Reflections from his Diaries
3 Ita Wegman and Karl König: Letters and Documents
4 The Child with Special Needs
5 Seeds for Social Renewal: The Camphill Village Conferences
6/7 The Calendar of the Soul: An Inner Journey through the Year
8 Becoming Human: A Social Task
9 Communities for Tomorrow
10 At the Threshold of the Modern Age: Biographies Around the Year 1861
11 Brothers and Sisters: The Order of Birth in the Family
12 Kaspar Hauser and Karl König
13 Animals: An Imaginative Zoology
14 Social Farming: Healing Humanity and the Earth
15 Nutrition from Earth and Cosmos
16 The Grail and the Development of Conscience
17 Plays for the Festivals of the Year
18 The Spirit of Camphill: Birth of a Movement
19 Stories, Poems and Meditations
20 Before Birth and Beyond Death: The Transformation of the Human Being
21 The Seasons and their Festivals: Human, Earthly and Cosmic Rhythms
22 The First Three Years of the Child
23 Music Therapy: Research and Insights
24 The Human Soul: Mysteries and Complexities of the Psyche
25 The Life of Karl König: Founder of the Camphill Movement

Karl König's collected works are being published in English by Floris Books and in German by Verlag Freies Geistesleben. They encompass the entire, wide-ranging literary estate of Karl König, including his books, essays, manuscripts, lectures, diaries, notebooks, his extensive correspondence and his artistic works, across twelve subjects.

Karl König Archive subjects

- Medicine and study of the human being
- Curative education and social therapy
- Psychology and education
- Agriculture and science
- Social questions
- The Camphill movement
- Christianity and the festivals
- Anthroposophy
- Spiritual development
- History and biographies
- Artistic and literary works
- Karl König's biography

Karl König Archive
www.karlkoeniginstitute.org
office@karlkoeniginstitute.org

www.ingramcontent.com/pod-product-compliance
Ingram Content Group UK Ltd.
Pitfield, Milton Keynes, MK11 3LW, UK
UKHW021620090826
474125UK00001B/20

9 781835 750131